LOOK BACK WITH JOY!

Newly-weds, Colin and Joy, 1939

LOOK BACK WITH JOY!

Memories from a full life in Africa—and beyond

by

JOY MOLYNEUX

Tentmaker Publications
121 Hartshill Road, Stoke-on-Trent, Staffs. ST4 7LU.

ISBN 1 899003 21 X

Cover:

Watercolour by Colin Arthur Molyneux

Table of Contents

PAGE

Chapter 1 The Early Days 9
Chapter 2 How It All Began 16
Chapter 3 The Valley of the Shadow of Death 22
Chapter 4 How a Slave became an Evangelist 28
Chapter 5 The Next Generation 32
Chapter 6 Booke 41
Chapter 7 Baby in a Box 48
Chapter 8 Tears and Triumphs of Medical Work 53
Chapter 9 Mother's Day 57
Chapter 10 God's Amazing Provision 61
Chapter 11 The Great Escape 65
Chapter 12 Encounter with the Lion 73
Chapter 13 When one Door Closes, Another Opens 83
Chapter 14 The Harvest is Over 88
Epilogue Look Forward with Joy! 95

PREFACE

"Joy, you really must write these stories down!"
"Joy, I wish my friend could have been with us today to hear all this! Is it in print anywhere?"

Time and time again, as I have spoken at women's meetings and church services around the country, people have urged me to put into writing my stories of God's faithfulness. Family members, too, sons and daughters-in-law, nephews and nieces, and (more recently) grandsons and granddaughters, have made similar appeals.

So, sharing the Psalmist's delight in declaring publicly God's wonderful deeds, I have put together the present little "book of remembrance" in the hope that it will encourage all who read it to "grow strong in faith". It should become obvious to all who read this book that it is really not about me but about our mighty Lord, who is the same yesterday, and today, and forever, and who is rich to *all* who call upon his name.

Many other people feature in these stories, and for all of them I want to thank God. The little book is dedicated to my late husband, Colin, with whom so many of these experiences were shared. I also want to thank my four sons and daughters-in-law, Colin and Christine, Malcolm and Elizabeth, Gordon and Christine, and David and Solweig for their constant encouragement in this project. My special thanks to Mu Miller for typing my handwritten maunuscripts and to my son Gordon for his work of editing. Without the help of all these, this would never have seen publication.

May God bless you as you read!

Editor's note: Over the last few months I have worked through the various stories, putting them in an appropriate order and eliminating undue repetition or overlap, and checking with my Mother about details and dates. But otherwise, I have sought to do the minimum possible so that Mother's style comes through clearly, and so that those who read the printed account will be able to "hear" Mother speaking in the graphic, enthusiastic way that they remember. (GM)

1

The Early Days

My early childhood as a missionaries' daughter prepared me for the life of a missionary wife and mother. My parents served in Angola, Portuguese West Africa, and I was born while they were still in Portugal learning the language. I was only three months old when I first arrived in Angola in 1915. In the course of many more years five brothers joined me in our family.

Accompanying our parents as they preached the Gospel amongst the local villages, our party would form a little caravan. Each child was carried in a hammock slung on a pole between two porters. The hammocks were shielded from the fierce sun by a canopy. The bearers enjoyed singing and chanting as they half-walked, half-jogged their way along the paths and through the forest. We children loved the swaying motion of the hammocks and we often joined in the singing. We taught them "It's a long way to Tipperary—it's a long way to go!" Our own English rendering was

"It's a long way to Heaven's glory!
It's a long way to go!
It's a long way to Jesus' country,
And God calls us to go!
Believe he died to save you—
'Tis very, very true
He wants to purify and heal us—
Just me and just you!"

This song, translated into the Chokwe language, was a great favourite on our safaris, and it led to the conversion of some of our porters!

One of my early memories was when I was only five. My father took me and my two little brothers to a village in the jungle. "Paramount Chief Mwatchiavwa is very ill. In fact he is on his deathbed. I want you to meet him." There he lay, a wizened old man lying on the leopard skin that marked his status as a chief, his head propped up on a low wooden block. In his time he had been an evil and dissolute man; in fact it was reported that he had even been a murderer. But in his final years he had come to faith in Jesus Christ as his Saviour, and now his face was open and kind.

"Chief Mwatchiavwa," my father asked gently, "Please will you tell my children why you are now not afraid of dying?"

The old chief looked at us and replied quietly but firmly, "Because I am hiding in the blood of Jesus."

Even at that young age of five, his words made a profound impression upon me. Two years later, when I was seven, I became a committed Christian. Our family were in Canada on leave. I was sharing a bed with a 9 year-old friend Dorothy. It was a stormy night, and I was lying awake terrified by the sound of the furious wind and sleet. I feared that Jesus might come that night,—and I was not ready! Vividly, I recalled Chief Mwatchiavwa's calm words, "I am hiding in the blood of Jesus, I am not afraid". Dorothy told me, "Just tell Jesus all about your sins. Thank Him that He died to take them all away." In my own simple way I did repent of my sin and trust Him. I slept peacefully through the rest of the night.

In the morning, Dorothy told me that I should share the good news of what happened in the night with my parents. I did. "Now I'm saved!" I told them triumphantly, and added, "And I want to be a missionary to Africa!" So my meeting with the old chief two years previous to that night was certainly a stepping stone towards my own faith in Christ. My conviction that I wanted to be a missionary grew with the passing days. I was going to train as a nurse and use that training in missionary service in Africa. Dorothy later became a missionary herself to the West Indies.

Later, in 1925, back in Angola, we acquired a Model T Ford, and the whole family set off eastward towards Northern Rhodesia (now Zambia), where I was to be left at boarding school. Through hundreds of miles of vast country and jungle there were no hotels or towns, so each night we had to camp in scrubland or forest. On one occasion my father enthused us to make a strong barricade enclosure with branches of thorn trees to protect us from the lions which were prowling around. We built a huge bonfire to scare them away. While we youngsters slept in or under the car, our parents kept vigil all night, because two lions were circling our camp. In fact, in the morning, they proudly showed us the footprints of these wild beasts. We were thrilled!

Eventually we reached our destination of Sakeji School. We were welcomed by the headmaster and the teacher, Mr. and Mrs. Judson. At first, they were the only teachers and I was the only pupil! The first real term started three months later in January, 1926, and six more pupils joined the 'student body'. However, the school soon gained momentum and before long we were quite a full complement. So began my first days at boarding school. I have happy memories of those years, especially when in due time my five brothers came as well, and we felt secure in each other's company. I can remember distinctly, one very quiet night, being suddenly awakened by a scuffling noise on the verandah of our dormitory – then a bang and a growl and the sound of something rushing off into the bush! In the morning it was discovered that a lion had come on to the verandah and eaten the saddle off the boys' bicycle and gone off with it! Hunters followed the spoor and eventually killed the lion only two miles away from our house. That story was written about and boasted about for weeks afterwards by all of us youngsters!

One other highlight I can remember was when we were all taken about 2½ miles off the beaten track into dense forest to see for ourselves the source of the great Zambezi River. Starting as a tiny rivulet in that remote spot in the very heart of Africa, the Zambezi steadily grows in volume, eventually plunging over the mighty Victoria Falls as it makes its long way to the Indian Ocean.

Some 25 years after I started at Sakeji School as the very first pupil, our own four sons enrolled there as second generation pupils. Many "Sakeji-ites" down through the years have in turn become themselves missionaries both in Africa and in other parts of the world.

So the years passed by. I did take my nurse's training and midwifery in London, with a view to becoming a missionary to Africa. Little did I know that in the same great city was a young man, Colin Molyneux, training at All Nations Christian College for work in Africa. We met, and our friendship grew as we realised what a lot we had in common, a deep love for God's work in Africa in a pioneer situation and a strong sense of call to missionary work. As our natural affection grew steadily into deep love, we began to have serious misgivings as to whether such a friendship was right! Should we not heed the Apostle Paul's warning to remain single, that we might devote ourselves the better to service in Africa?

We prayed earnestly together and separately about this. One afternoon we visited a Bible bookshop in Exeter, and while browsing around admiring the display of books, we were suddenly arrested by a beautiful plaque which read:

"Take Joy home, and make a place
In thy great heart for her,
And love and cherish her
And she shall come and sing to thee
When thou art working in the furrows."

— Anon.

Joy, the first pupil at Sakeji School, 1925

Leonard & Lillian Gammon and family (Joy on the right)

Our hands met, and our eyes too! Surely God was telling us quite plainly that this friendship was all in His great plan! He had called us, trained us, and now caused us to meet! In just the same way Jesus had called His disciples to go out in His Name. He had sent them forth two by two to go wherever He went. He also assured US that as we sought Him and His Kingdom FIRST, He would see to all other things. Praise God! What love welled up in our hearts for Him and for each other. Of course, we'd love to go together—no doubt about that! We were married on December 19th, 1939, in Cape Town.

A few months later we were settling in the Congo, in the heart of the equatorial forest, in a very remote area. We set about learning the language of Lingala, in order to be able to communicate with the people and to tell them of the Gospel of our Lord Jesus Christ, which was the main reason why we had come. After two years, Colin John (the first of our four sons), was born. This event caused great excitement in the villages around, and for the next few weeks we had crowds of people coming to see the new white baby. In the course of the next eight years, three more sons were born.

But the story is running away with me! Here I must interrupt and explain how it all began.

2

How it all began

In 1889 William Gammon was a young teacher in a public school in Cambridge. He was doing very well outwardly, but inwardly was full of doubts and fears. Life seemed hopeless, purposeless and dull. Feeling increasingly depressed he went to hear a lecture by F. B. Meyer, an eminent preacher, at a men's meeting in a local church. This preacher was a man full of the Holy Spirit and power. He spoke eloquently about God's amazing love and salvation, and insisted that those of us who have eternal life must pass it on to others. As William listened, he was convinced that God was speaking directly to him. When the final hymn was sung, William joined in with deep emotion:—

When I survey the wondrous Cross
On which the King of Glory died,
My richest gain I count but loss
And pour contempt on all my pride.

Love so amazing, so divine,
Demands my heart, my life, my all.

"If you meant what you were singing," said Mr. Meyer, "sing from your heart:—

Love so amazing, so divine,
Shall have my heart, my life, my all."

William sang, because he knew that from this moment he would devote his life to God's service. There had been a transformation in his heart.

A short time later, back in Devon, William was at the bedside of his mother, who was dying. Kneeling beside her, he told her of this recent experience and that he wished to be a missionary in Africa – to devote his life to telling Africans about God's salvation. She gave him her blessing, saying that to serve God was life's highest calling.

At about this same time, William's father, a devout Christian, attended a Missionary Conference in Exeter, where a great pioneer missionary, Fred Stanley Arnot, was bringing an appeal for young men and women to go as 'messengers of the Cross' to Africa. Towards the close of the meeting, they sang Isaac Watts' great hymn "When I survey the wondrous Cross". The whole congregation was deeply moved as they sang this wonderful hymn together. Arnot broke in towards the end to say, "The last words of this hymn are: –

> Love so amazing, so divine,
> Demands my heart, my life, my all…,

but if you yourself cannot go out as a missionary, are you willing to send one of your own children? If so, sing: –

> Love so amazing, so divine,
> *Shall have my sons, my life, my all!"*

Mr. Gammon, who had married twice and had twelve sons and daughters, sang those very words from a full heart and with deep emotion, and really meant them. He knew it was a great honour to give his all to God.

William and his father were later amazed to find that they had been led by God into a deep commitment to give and to go without reserve in different towns and on different days, but by the same hymn! No wonder that hymn has meant so much to the family ever since.

William did eventually go out to Africa as a missionary.

He served God there for only 2 years, for during a severe tropical storm he was struck by lightning. He suffered badly during the last painful days of his life, and died from extensive burns and shock. But before he died, William told the missionaries at his bedside that he had no regrets—he loved Africa and its people, and counted it a great privilege to serve them. In his last letter to his family in England he appealed to them, *"Still keep up the old interest in Africa. Never be daunted either to send or to help because of my leaving the field so quickly. But I triumph still, and thank the Lord for any testimony he has let me bear for Him in this dark and lovely land of Africa. I wish you all Goodbye – Will."*

He died in February 1898, aged 27 years, and was buried in Northern Rhodesia (now Zambia).

Many years elapsed. From the triumph of William's death, three more Gammons soon went out to Africa: his sisters, Annie, Dora, and Leonard. So began the far-reaching ministry of one family and their children and grandchildren. Leonard, above mentioned, was only 17 when his brother William died so tragically. He was deeply challenged by William's last letter, and by the fact that his two sisters had responded to the tragedy by going themselves out to Rhodesia and Angola. Leonard continued his studies and qualified as an analytical chemist and got a good job in Exeter. But he had no peace in his heart until he said to God, "Here am I, Lord, send me." So in 1909 he, too, sailed for Angola and joined his sister Annie and other missionaries at Capango in Bie Province, where they established a strong church and medical and school work. He learned the difficult Umbundu language "on his knees", because he maintained it was only by prayer that he would ever master it.

A couple of years prior to this, across the Atlantic in the USA, a young lady called Lillian Boggess had attended a meeting where a missionary couple from Africa, Mr. and Mrs. Taylor, were showing lantern slides of their work in Angola. Lillian's great Aunt Abigail had been a very enthusiastic missionary throughout her long life, and Lillian often conversed with her about Christian service. That evening Lillian was deeply moved by one slide which was left in position for a long time, the missionary saying, "Look at these faces, – dark and appealing! These people have never yet heard the Gospel of Jesus our Saviour!" That one slide riveted itself in her memory, and she prayed, "Lord, send me to those Chokwe people, – please!" Not long after that she went out to Africa with the Taylors, and immediately loved the people and set to learning their language. However, as often in missionary service, there was a severe test of faith for missionaries – a desperate famine descended on Chokweland, and the missionaries were advised to leave. However, they thought they must pray especially and ask God what they should do. He gave them a command and a promise: – Psalm 37.3 – "Trust in the Lord and do good; dwell in the land and surely you will be fed." What more could they want? They stayed right there for many years and "did good" – building up the church, school and medical work and establishing a healthy community of African Christians.

Not long after Leonard arrived in Angola, he attended a conference of missionaries in that region, and there he met the lovely Canadian-born Lillian Boggess! Leonard and Lillian became well acquainted during the conference, and he was deeply impressed with her 'happy and confident' nature. This friendship grew to a deep love and admiration for each other, as they shared how God had prepared them for His call to Africa. Her family had all originated in England and were devout Christians, greatly influenced by George Müller of Bristol, Frances Ridley Havergal, and the missionary Hudson Taylor. John and Caroline Townsend, her great-grandparents, had a large family and were zealous for God and His work. The whole family emigrated to U.S.A. in the early 1800s and settled in Buffalo, in New York State.

Before she died, Caroline Townsend made it her fervent

prayer that there would be a Christian missionary in every generation of her family.

Leonard and Lillian subsequently returned to USA to get married, amongst her large family, and they spent their leave visiting many churches. Then they travelled to England to meet Leonard's family and churches. Angola being a Portuguese colony in those days, they had to spend several months in Portugal. It was during that period their first baby was born, Joy Townsend Gammon (author of this book). Why did they call her Joy? Because Lillian had a long and weary labour, and she was weeping with frustration and pain. The reading for that night was Psalm 30 verse 5—"Weeping may endure for a night, but joy cometh in the morning!" Lillian smiled through her tears and exclaimed "if it's a girl, we'll call her Joy", and so they did.

Together Leonard and Lillian thanked God for this lovely gift from Him, and dedicated this first baby to the Lord. But the test of faith came, for the baby cried so much, and Lillian was inexperienced. She cried "Lord, this gift has become a great burden—please help!" When Leonard came in they opened their Bible for a promise and comfort. Psalm 55 verse 20 stood out for them—"Cast thy burden upon the Lord, and He shall sustain you." The margin of this Bible gave as an alternative translation of 'burden'—'gift'! Yes, even God's gifts to us can become a burden, but, cast upon the Lord they are transformed. Lillian and Leonard's hearts were encouraged, and the baby became more manageable. How often God's word comes just when we need it urgently. They returned together to the Chokwe country where they served God amongst very needy people.

So it was there in Chokweland that Leonard and Lillian brought up their family. I and my five brothers all lived there during our formative years (the first brother, David, died tragically as a young man, following an operation in hospital).

And so, to rejoin the story of Chapter 1, many years later

I became myself in turn a missionary to Africa, and my brothers Walter, Alan, Theo and Philip all became Christian missionaries to different parts of Africa and America.

Leonard and his sisters Annie and Dora all served God for many years. In the course of time they were all buried in their chosen land of Africa—just as their older brother William had been before them, whose tragic death was to have such far-reaching and fruitful repercussions!

God's ways are indeed wonderful!

3

The Valley of the Shadow of Death

Yes, God's ways are wonderful, but that does not mean that those who trust Him have no problems or difficulties. Indeed God often allows His children to go through times of deep testing and weakness in which they learn to trust Him and prove His faithfulness in ways which otherwise would not be possible.

In March 1942 Colin and I went through a most horrible experience together—yet with a happy ending. We had only been married a short time, and our firstborn, Colin John, was only six months old when it happened. Having just returned from an exhausting safari in the dense tropical jungle visiting many African villages, we returned to the mission to recuperate and also continue our usual busy programme.

Suddenly my husband went down seriously ill with severe headaches and high fever and rigours—the dreaded malaria! In spite of our treatment and intensive care, we nurses could not get the temperature down, and Colin collapsed. But God heard our desperate cry for help. Shortly after the episode, Colin himself wrote to his parents in England the following graphic account of facing death—and coming back! It was later made into a leaflet and was the means of challenging many readers. It is reproduced here in full:—

Afraid to Die?

by
Rev. Colin A. Molyneux

We got back from that trek I told you about on Tuesday, full of plans of all that we were going to do: school, Bible school, baptisms, buildings and what not. But God had other and better plans, of which we knew nothing.

On the Thursday night I went down with malaria, which later proved to be the first really bad attack I've had so far. On Friday and Saturday my temperature soared up to nearly 105 degrees in spite of maximum doses of quinine. Nothing, it seemed, would bring down this obstinate fever, and the large doses of quinine provided me with unceasing music in my ears day and night – not for a moment did it abate, till I felt almost at nerves' end. If I did drop off to sleep it was to land in a nightmare.

On Sunday things were much the same, but in the afternoon something happened. What it was I don't think I know. Joy had gone out of the room for a little while, and suddenly I had the strangest conviction – premonition – that I have ever had in my life; and as my wife came back into the room just then I told her that my end had come. She sent a message quickly to the other missionaries, and at that time I knew I was sinking fast. My feet and legs were quite cold and stiff, and so were my fingers and hands – quite cold and numb, so that I couldn't move them. Miss Baker, the other nurse here, gave me an injection of caffeine, and while it helped for a time, it was not long before I had sunk so low again that my heart seemed almost to have stopped, and, as Joy and Miss Baker afterwards confirmed, my pulse was only a thread. I felt that each breath was going to be my last. By this time I had said Goodbye to all the others, sent parting messages to all of you (you know what they were, I think, without my writing them down), took one last farewell of my beloved Joy, and then gave myself up to pass away from this world into Heaven.

Here I want to stop to say that death, as I found, to one who is trusting in the Lord Jesus Christ, has no fear whatsoever. Often I've read about it – often I've sung about it; but that has carried little weight with me. Now I KNOW, for I have been to the very gate of death and I have proved that Jesus Christ, the Son of God, has removed all the sting from death for those who love and follow Him. I tell you this because I want you to know from the experience of one who has been there, that at the end of life there is nothing to fear, but rather a joyous expectation of meeting with Christ face to face at any moment. It was a wonderful experience to me to be able to prove in actual fact that death is, to the Christian, a time of peace, of joy, of triumph.

But as I lay there, almost gone, one other thought came to me as clearly: I'm just going from the world out into Eternity; whatever must it be for one who has no assurance of Heaven, who in his life has never stopped to think of eternity, who has trusted in his own goodness of life? In that moment I saw what one's own goodness is like as one prepares to go into eternity, and in that same brief moment, I shuddered at the thought of the very agony of one who comes to his last breath – too late now to think of beginning to prepare oneself, too late now to ask help of another – one more second and it will be eternity! Oh, it was ghastly! – and no words I can write now can convey to you anything of the terror and dread urgency that I visualised in that awful moment. Yes, when you come to think of it, death is real; not the nebulous, far-off thing that foolish ones think it to be in their health and pleasure-seeking: no, it is very real and very near to every one of us, and to come up to the very brink of it without Christ, having neglected His offer of pardon and salvation, is an agony greater than any other that we can know in this world. Never shall I forget the appalling gloom of that vision, as I sank, so I thought, into the joys of an Eternity with Christ.

While it seemed hopeless, Joy had not lost hope, and called for an intramuscular injection, followed soon afterwards by another intravenous, and for a while it seemed that the crisis had passed as

I began to rally a little, and it began to look as though I might get through. There followed a sleepless night, and early the next morning the missionaries despatched a cyclist to our nearest neighbours calling for help. He had been gone barely an hour when again I felt my heart beginning to fail. All the previous days' symptoms returned, but now it was worse, for after that the end was inevitable, for even the injections had failed and there was nothing left.

As I was once more preparing to "depart this life", Joy suddenly bent over me and said, "Wouldn't you like us to pray for you?" "Yes", I said, "I would." They gathered round. "And would you like us to anoint you with oil, as the Bible says?" (James 5.14-16). "Yes", I said, "by all means." John Scheepers thereupon anointed my head with oil and prayed the prayer of faith, as we are exhorted in this passage I have just mentioned. The five of us were now deliberately and definitely trusting the Lord Jesus to save my life, although everything pointed to the hopelessness of it. We prayed, we trusted, we received in faith, but still no evidence of any healing from God. Rather I felt even weaker, if possible. Incidentally, at this time about 10 Africans were gathered silently in prayer outside the house.

Time and again I felt myself going, but Joy's amazing assurance of faith seemed just to keep me alive. Once in fact I thought (and they thought) I had just about gone, when Joy emphatically declared, "No Colin, you are not going! God has given me the assurance that you will live." What was to be done? We had asked the Lord and we had trusted, but nothing had happened. And then Joy said that we ought to start praising the Lord in faith for having raised me up. And so they all began praising and thanking God for the wonderful deliverance yet unseen. And as they praised and I praised – into my body there flowed new life from God. I knew it and they saw it.

Then, my life saved, God suddenly poured down upon us all a deep conviction of sin, and as they knelt around the bed, and I lay upon the bed, God spoke to each heart, and one by one we were broken down before the Lord as He reminded us of words of criticism and thoughts harboured against others of His children. What a time we had around that bed! We had never been in such a meeting before. Blessed though the fellowship had been amongst the missionaries before, it was now something deeper than we had ever known. And so God saved my life when medicines had all seemed to fail, and it was not long afterwards that Joy was changing me – so much stronger had I become.

Joy and I had never been very earnest proclaimers of the power of God to heal the physical body, and while we'd often said, Yes, God could heal, yet we had no vital experience of His power in this way. But now we can tell others with full assurance, even as the Bible proclaims, that the Lord can and does heal the physical body quite apart from medicines. At this time all my troubles seemed to be going rapidly, my heart was stronger, my fever, at last, was down, and the big blotchy sores that decorated my face began rapidly to heal. Oh, how wonderful it all was! And it has made the Lord Jesus more real and more dear to me than ever before. We shall, of course, still take quinine regularly; nor have we discarded medicines "lock, stock and barrel" for we know God often uses them; but we also know now that the power of God can raise us even from death, if need be, without medicine. So praise the Lord with me!

None of our readers will gather from this, we trust, that God is necessarily bound always to act in this way. Our life and death are in His sovereign hands, and we must ever submit to His perfect will.

Actually, my husband Colin had not enjoyed good health as a young man. He had been advised to stay off vigorous sport, and his weak heart had meant that professional medical advice did not encourage him to embark on missionary service in Central Africa. He fell victim quite often to malaria while in the Congo. But it is a testimony to the sustaining power of God that he not only completed 21 years there, but followed that with 16 years of service with the International Nepal Fellowship as General Secretary based in UK, and lived until 1989, when he died at the age of 78.

4

How a Slave became an Evangelist

Amongst our earliest converts at Booke Mission was a dirty and scruffy young fellow of about 20 years old from a despised slave-tribe. His name was Bosau (pronounced Boo-Sow). From the moment he trusted God to save him, and he was sure he was a NEW man in Christ, he declared that his new name would be Paul—and so from then on he grew in grace and in the knowledge of God.

I knew there was a radical change in Bosau, because he was eager to learn all he could, and his first request from me was for soap, "to make my body as clean as my heart is now!" From then on he was alert and energetic, and always clean and tidy. We rejoiced at the transforming power of God in his whole attitude. Coming into our Bible school and learning quickly and thoroughly, he absorbed all that we and the Word of God could teach him......but he had not found a Christian girl to marry, so that together they could carry the Good News to the villages that had never heard of Christ.

On occasions, Bosau and I prayed about this serious problem. We remembered that Abraham had sent his trusted servant to a far country to get a bride for his beloved son Isaac—and this man had asked God for wisdom and insight, and God wonderfully answered his prayer. He came back with lovely Rebecca—who was just right for Isaac. "Could God do that for me?" asked Paul.

The long vacation came, and Bosao set forth to his "far country" to visit his relatives scattered through the Ndengese Region and get from them gifts towards the dowry for his bride-to-be. Great faith! In the meanwhile we missionaries had arranged a special evangelistic mission in several villages within an easy radius of the large village of Kokitale. Grace Baker and I were the missionaries, with one African evangelist couple accompanying us for two weeks. God wonderfully blessed that mission, and we had excellent attendances and splendid singing. Quite a number of young and old, men and women, came to trust Christ as Saviour, notably several teenage girls, one a fine girl called Amba. We gave them many extra counselling meetings, and left the evangelist and his wife there in Kokitale to teach these new believers about God and His Word. The response was quite remarkable. The next two months saw the establishing of the church in Kokitale, and the converts were joyous and real, and we missionaries went to Kokitale for extra visits too.

The long vacation was drawing to its close, and Bosao Paul, having acquired quite a few "riches" (beads, earrings, bracelets and money) toward the bride price, was still praying for his elusive wife! He continued on the long line of villages until late one afternoon he sat wearily on a fallen log outside Kokitale village to read his Bible and pray, not knowing where he would lodge that night. Hearing the approaching voices of girls singing songs about fishing and hunting, he prayed in his heart earnestly—"Lord, if she (my Christian bride-to-be) is in this group, please tell her to offer me some fish!" Along the path came ten or twelve young damsels all carrying waterpots on their heads, and bundles of fish in their hands—singing merrily because of their successful fishing. As Amba, an eighteen-year-old girl, came opposite Paul she exclaimed, "You must be a Christian—you are reading God's Word in our language!"

"Yes, indeed, I am a Christian going back to Bible School

at the Mission—and will be going to Booke Mission tomorrow."

"Well", declared Amba, "you must have a fish supper with my father and mother and me tonight." Paul's heart leapt for joy. God had answered his prayer—fish for supper and a Christian girl.

Over supper she told how God had transformed her life and saved her during the mission two months ago. Since then her parents had called off the engagement they had arranged for her, as was their custom, and realized she would now only marry a committed Christian. It didn't take long for Bosao Paul to know that he and Amba were meant for each other, just as Isaac and Rebecca had been chosen by God. They were married later on and Amba joined her husband in the Bible School training. So the slave boy Bosao became Evangelist Paul and together he and Amba made an excellent partnership.

They were assigned to their first village, Kokitale, and had a fruitful ministry there. Also I had the joy of helping Amba with their first baby's arrival—dear little Joseph, just like his dad! Praise God.

Paul and Amba had a second baby, unfortunately born dead—and this caused great grief and a test of faith for this dear couple. Their heathen relatives were indignant that Paul would not consent to the rituals usually performed on dead babies so that witchcraft powers could bring back this baby in another form later. Amba and Paul refused, and conducted a normal Christian burial—but this caused a great deal of friction for quite a while. They stood their ground, saying that God in good time would give them another baby.

By this time Amba and Paul had been transferred, with little Joseph to the village of Nkile, and had many joys in their work for God, but also considerable opposition from unbelievers. However, God blessed their work, and a small church was formed at Nkile. Before long Amba was expecting again, much to their joy and delight. Satan knows how to attack and challenge, and Amba had a difficult labour, with only African midwives attending. Paul prayed earnestly for God to work a miracle for them and deliver his wife of a live child.

Meanwhile, Colin and I were all packed for a two-day trek through to the north to help a missionary couple, the wife being very ill and needing nursing. As we stood ready to leave on our bicycles, and the porters tying up loads, a cyclist came panting into the mission, with an urgent letter—"Don't come, please, because the missionary couple have had to go quickly to the doctor!" We were baffled! Ready to leave at once—and now what an anti-climax! We and the other missionaries prayed to God to show us what we were to do! We prayed for a while, asking God to reveal His plan.

God gave us a mounting conviction that we should go to Nkile,—in the opposite direction! Immediately we got on the bikes and together with our porters set forth for Nkile, assuredly gathering that something special awaited us.

We arrived at the outskirts of Nkile to see our dear friend Paul pacing up and down in a desperate way, crying. When he saw us he shouted "Praise God! He has heard and answered our prayers!" We soon saw to poor Amba's desperate need, and not more than two hours later, a happy and relaxed group of relatives were thanking God for delivering safely another baby boy into the arms of Bosao, whose joy knew no bounds! Little Samuel became a living example of God's miraculous intervention in a desperate situation. We stayed for several days at Nkile and several dear African people came to know Jesus as their Saviour and Healer! Praise God!

5

The Next Generation

All four of our sons (Colin John, Malcolm, Gordon, and David) were born while we were at Booke, a remote mission post some 300 miles north of Luluabourg in the North Sankuru district of the Kasai in Central Congo. This was the world they came to regard as home: dense jungle, equatorial rainforest climate (hot and sticky), no electricity or running water, but plenty of adventure and freedom from restrictions of Western life.

As the years flew by, our big problem was how to get the boys educated. My old school Sakeji in Northern Zambia naturally came to our minds, but it was 1250 miles away!

Our two older sons, Colin John and Malcolm, were 8 and 6 when we first had to make that trip to Sakeji. The journey by truck took us five days, starting on Monday morning at 6 a.m., spending each night at a different mission station, and arriving at the school on Saturday morning. Colin John and Malcolm were going to school for the first time, and Gordon, who was only 3½, went along with us. Also I was expecting my fourth child! We tried to make the journey interesting for the children by telling exciting stories, each taking part by telling a few sentences at a time, then pouncing on someone else to continue! This whiled away the long hours of driving, kept us all alert—and gave us a good deal of fun. It also gave our boys valuable experience in telling a story in an animated way—good practice for future preaching!

We would drive into the school on the Saturday morning,

Almost at the end of our 1,250 mile journey
to Sakeji School. (1953?)
L-R: Malcolm, Colin-John, Gordon, David with Mum and Dad.

Mission personnel at Booke (c. 1946)
Colin & Joy on right, with Colin-John, Malcolm and Gordon (in arms). Next to Colin is Aunty Ko.

arriving at the same time as a small crowd of other missionaries and their children, and of course there was much talking to old and new friends from all over that part of Africa. This was the time for settling up our school fees with the Headmaster, and it was wonderful how God supplied this particular need always in advance of each term. We spent the last precious Sunday all together—parents and children mingling for Church service and general fellowship, and looking around the school grounds and surrounding country. Monday came. Farewells and prayers were said with our dear boys, and then—the hard bit—a hasty get-away. We were assured by the Staff that tears were soon replaced by activity and busyness, and most children soon settled to routine and lots to do! The policy at Sakeji School was to give the children a full programme of activity in school and play, gardening and hobbies of all sorts, so that there was little time for homesickness! But for some especially it was painful, and all the children had to learn to lean upon the Lord for His help and His comfort when the way was hard. We adults did the same!

I recall my husband telling the two boys to remember when they were in bed, five lovely words that Jesus said—I will never leave thee "Even in the dark you can say the words on one hand, starting with the big thumb—I (Jesus) will never leave you!" This was a real comfort to them both. Colin John exclaimed "Yes, Daddy, and you can say it another way, starting with the little finger—"*I* will never leave *You* (Lord)". That double meaning meant a lot to us all.

The children were of course taken for swimming, football, tennis, rounders and gymnastics, and lessons were made as interesting as possible. Since travel distances were so vast and had to be made by road, there were two terms instead of the usual three. The long terms meant that separation was more painful, but conversely, the reunion at the end of term was more euphoric. There was another advantage, too. Each 4½ month term was punctuated by two half terms instead of just one, and comprised all sorts of adventures and enjoyable activities like floating down the stream on inflated inner-tubes, or having "supper-in-bags" in the open air.

When the 18-week term eventually came to its end, Colin and I once more set out on the Monday morning from Booke to collect the two boys,—this time with four-year old Gordon and our new baby brother David as well! Great excitement when our vehicle drove into Sakeji compound with baby David to be admired by all!

As we drove out of Sakeji for the holidays—what excitement and joy, as we realised that we were together again, and we all began singing our favourite song in jubilant mood—

"Home we go, home we go!
End of term—jolly good show!
From all of our lessons there comes a release
And Daddy's just gone off to warn the police!
Home we go! Home we go!
Whether it's sunshine or rain
But we must remember, sometime in September
To jolly well come back again!"

And so began the long journey across plains, through savannah scrubland and forest, across rivers on rickety bridges or "pontoons" (ferries made out of a platform of planks carried on dugout canoes or iron floats), through thick sand (if it was dry) or slimy mud (when rain was pouring down!) or dreadfully stony roads and rough tracks—all had to be traversed. There was even one stretch of road "paved" entirely with palmnut kernels discarded from a local Lever Bros. palm-oil factory. One of the exciting pastimes was when a large cushion was placed on Daddy's knee "at the wheel" and each boy had a chance to drive the car!

So these trips were made to and from Booke Mission to

Sakeji School to enable our boys to spend two long holidays each year with us away up in Central Congo. As the boys grew older Gordon joined the other two at Sakeji. David was *very* impatient to join his brothers at school. Every time we went, he protested loudly and bitterly that he wanted to stay at Sakeji too! Of course, all too soon he was six years old, and then it was all four who were left at Sakeji. On that first occasion especially in Colin's and my heart there was a dread and sadness—how could we bear to part with *all* of them at once! Furthermore, we were anxious because we had the fees for three—but not for four. We never shared this with the children but as we drove we made this financial need an urgent matter for prayer. How often we had claimed the promise, "My God shall supply all your need!" How often we had proved it to be true. But there had been nothing in the last mail delivery. We stopped at the General Post Office in our nearest town of Luluabourg, hoping that perhaps we would find there the answer to our prayer. But nothing. What a test of faith! Arriving at the school, we were given the usual noisy and hilarious welcome by children and parents. In the general hubbub, the Headmaster handed Colin a letter which had been forwarded from England (it had been six weeks coming!). In that one and only letter was a cheque more than enough to cover David's fees for the coming term and our travelling expenses back! Praise God! That was the only occasion we received money actually at the school! It was an extra bonus, and once again proof of God's faithfulness to us.

So *all four* boys were left at school, and Colin and I felt forlorn as we drove away from Sakeji to start the long journey back in a silent car. I remember suddenly bursting out in tears and saying, "Oh it's *so* hard! One of them might even die before we could hear they were ill!" Mail took so long to reach us in those early days. We dried our tears and pressed on!

Back at the mission station again we set to work with the school, teaching the African boys and girls in Lingala or in French, caring for the sick (and, in my case, doing midwifery) and working in the Bible School also. Those were busy days, and priority No.1 was the weekly letter to our four dear boys at school. They also wrote to us each Sunday, supervised by a teacher. So we kept in touch by letters and much prayer. That first term with all four of our boys away for over four months seemed extra long, I remember. However, the day came when we set off once more early on a Monday morning to fetch the lads. Were we excited! Arrangements were made *en route* to stay one week on the return journey in a mission guest house by Lake Munkamba, a favourite holiday spot with a bilharzia-free lake—excellent for swimming and boating. Eventually on the Saturday morning our car drew into Sakeji compound, with whoops of delight from four very excited boys—"Oh, you didn't tell us we have a new car!! What make is it?" (a second-hand Plymouth Station Wagon, admired and loved at first sight!) This was the "secret" we had told them of in our last two letters, and they were delighted. There were hugs and kisses and excited exclamations.

As usual, early Monday morning saw us pull out of Sakeji on the return journey. When we had crossed a certain rickety bridge some distance away from Sakeji we considered that our holidays had really started. We would stop briefly on the road, switch off the engine, and thank God for all His love and protection for us since we were last together; we would also commit the journey ahead to God. Then the engine was started, the horn joyously tooted three times, and off we went!

The second day of our journey was through exceptionally dense jungle, with a large river to cross by pontoon. On one such occasion, as we drove on, we all became aware of a sound of rhythmic chanting and drumming and stamping of feet even over the noise of the engine. As we came alongside we could see a huge circle of dancing men in a roadside clearing. Their bodies were clothed with animal skins, on their ankles they had strings of shells or seed-pods, and they were brandishing double-sided daggers! Stopping the car, we all walked over to the dancers, fascinated by their movements and the noise. They seemed to take no notice of us, but gradually the circles of dancers closed around us. The deafening noise of stamping and the sight of their glistening, perspiring bodies was impressive. We were all transfixed by the scene with a mixture of excitement and terror.

Suddenly Colin and I felt a strong warning in our hearts – "There is something evil and sinister here. Come! we must go!!" We made our way as quickly as possible back to the car and sped towards the mission 20 miles further on, where we were staying the night. Over supper we all excitedly told about the scene we had been in. "Oh," said the missionaries, "You were in great danger there. On a particular day each year that ceremony takes place. Those men dance on and on in ever increasing frenzy, helped on by strong drink – and about midnight they select a human victim, kill him and eat him!" We were amazed and silenced, realizing that the "inner warning" was God's goodness and protection.

You ask, "Why on earth did you take the children to such an outlandish place so far away from home?" The answer is that Sakeji School in Zambia was the only school for missionaries' children which catered for British children, though there was an excellent American school in the Congo. The English curriculum was essential for their education. The dedication of the staff at the school, and the discipline and spiritual training provided an excellent foundation for further education. Many of the children from Sakeji went on in later years to be missionaries, too. In the staff meetings the children were prayed for by name, and we parents appreciated this. Because of this school, many missionaries were able to continue their service for God in Africa. In our own case, because of Sakeji School we were able to spend 10 extra years at Booke Mission, knowing that our boys were being cared for and educated in a healthy part of Africa.

At the close of their last term at the school, Colin and Malcolm were two of four young people baptised in the Sakeji River by my husband Colin. The baptisms were followed by a wonderful communion service held in a full church with African and white folk worshipping together, and singing lustily "To God be the Glory—great things He hath done!"

6

Booke

Our mission base of Booke (pronounced Baw-kee) was more or less on the equator and was situated on a hill overlooking a deep and wide valley full of dense tropical trees and vegetation. A clearing about a mile square had been made by cutting down enormous trees—about a thousand in all—taking out all the roots and levelling the ground before building the four houses and one church. No small task. In fact, that job took three years to accomplish.

The established mission station now looked beautiful, with green lawns all round the houses, and bougainvillaea and hibiscus, as well as tall palm trees. Frequent and heavy rainfall kept everything green and lush. Below us in the valley we could often hear the crashing of elephants, chatter of monkeys, and the occasional growl of leopards. There were many snakes and small animals too.

One hundred African schoolboys lived in dormitories up the road, and attended school daily, with missionaries and two trained African teachers in charge. As these 10-18 year old boys had no school background and were totally unused to school discipline, the staff had a big job on their hands, and much wisdom and patience were needed. School was given only four days a week, Wednesday and Saturday being free for hunting for food or going home to the nearby villages to visit families and friends. So Wednesday was a welcome break. The day started with 6.30 a.m. "Assembly" in the chapel, where about 100 young voices heartily sang hymns in the Lingala language and a short gospel message was preached. Each day emphasised one special verse from the Word of God, repeated several times by the whole congregation to memorise it. And then,—off on the hunt. We missionaries enjoyed the respite, and used the day for medical work, correspondence, carpentry and household duties. We cheerfully waved from the veranda while the long procession of fellows gradually and noisily disappeared from sight in the dense foliage ....praying in our hearts that they would all return safely in the evening!

So the busy day wore on until we were glad to hear a noisy but exhausted gang returning from the hunt with several animals they had killed—it might be two large antelopes, one tortoise, perhaps even a young leopard. They were pleased and proud, and marched jauntily up the road to their houses to prepare for a good feast!

But, on one such occasion, Ntangeli the head teacher came down with an anxious face. He had checked his register and found to his horror that five boys had not returned with the crowd—each group had thought they were with the other. There was nothing for it but for Ntangeli to go with one senior lad and search for the five lost ones. The hurricane lamp was immediately lit to its highest pressure and we waved the two young men off, with a strong prayer to God for their success. We watched from the veranda as they walked purposefully down into the dense underbrush. Very soon the blackness engulfed all light from the pressure lamp. Darkness was rapidly blotting out the lovely red afterglow of sunset .... and the jungle reverberated with the incessant buzz of insects and night birds.

In the meanwhile, our two searchers were making their way as quickly as possible stalking through difficult terrain, but the lamp showed up, all along the trail, the chinks and scars on trees that the hunt leader had made that morning! What a tremendous help that was! Eerie shadows and animal calls

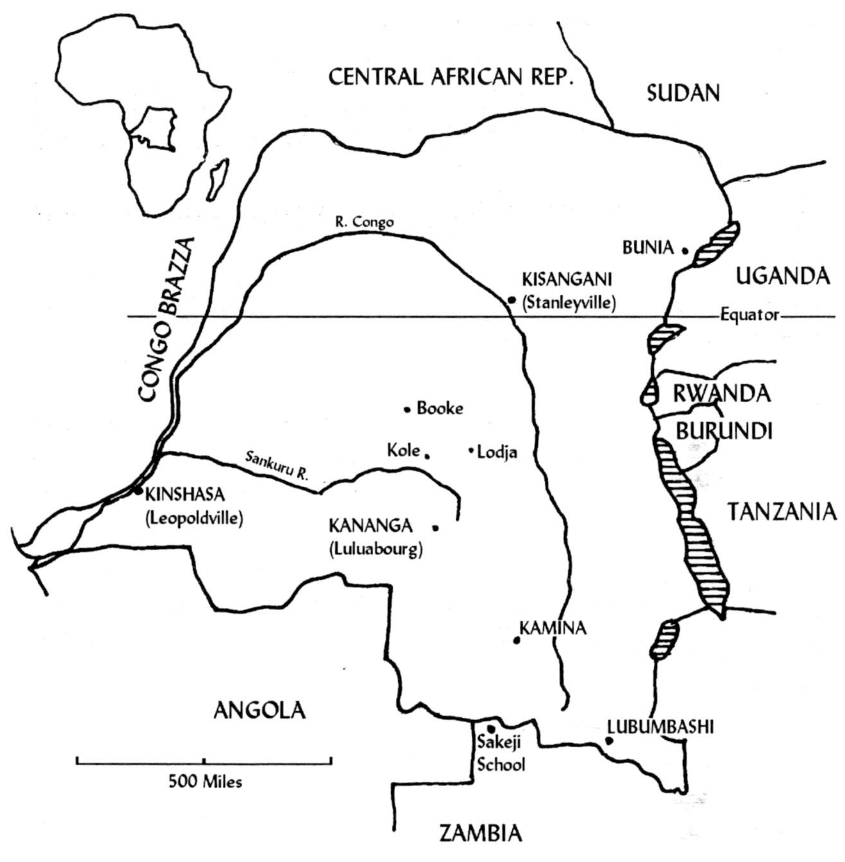

MAP of CONGO

made them alert and ready for anything and as they went they were calling—"Boys, where are you....?" Then they would stand still and listen intently. Nothing! On they went, crashing and stumbling, and calling again and again. The humidity and chill of the atmosphere added to their feeling of anxiety and apprehension, but they hesitated a moment. Yes, voices were heard crying for help. Thank God! Soon they came upon the five lads huddled together shivering from cold and fright. In the bright beam of the light they looked like caged animals—

petrified, then relieved beyond words! No time for excuses or explanations. The small group followed the teachers and the bright light. "Follow closely, or you will be lost in the dark. Keep close to the light!"

Soon the seven were standing, exhausted but happy, back on the Mission on the hill. They were later reprimanded, but reunited with all their friends. All this made wonderful fuel for Colin's sermon in assembly the next morning! Jesus said, "I am the light of the world; he who follows me will not walk in darkness, but shall have the light of life!" — life eternal in Christ Jesus.

This became our theme song. Praise God!

Christian missionaries are those who have heard the call of God to "go into all the world and preach the Gospel" of Jesus Christ the Saviour, through several "channels" — evangelism, medical work, teaching, and practical and technical training. All these means are used in order to bring about the goal of a Christian church.

The mission leader (for Congo) had to have an excellent knowledge of French in order to attend to matters of state, with government officials and bureaucracy. We often had government officials visit the mission to see what we were actually achieving — some were friendly, others just the opposite. We had to be hospitable and polite with all of them! This was Colin's role.

Those involved in school teaching had to have a good knowledge of the local language and a sympathetic understanding of the people themselves in order to convey secular knowledge and spiritual. French was also taught in our schools, but few of our missionaries were proficient in both French and Lingala. The teacher was hard-pressed and needed much patience, but results were very encouraging, because most of the boys were eager to learn and 'get on in the world'. Discipline and order were a priority — and we were very encouraged with progress made over the years.

Some of our Senior boys (17-20 year olds) when they became keen Christians, came later into our Bible school. A school assembly was attended by everybody from 6-6.30 a.m., followed by two hours manual work, such as cutting firewood and stacking it in the shed; fetching water, making bricks and mortar for future building.

The paid workmen had tasks such as sawing boards from large trees, felling trees in the forest, building houses, splitting the soft wood of the *bichumbe* tree into tiles for roofs, etc. All these tasks were done under supervision, and much valuable experience learned by all! At 9 a.m.a drum was beaten to inform all that there was one hour's break for a meal—and missionaries and workforce escaped to their dwellings to relax and eat.

In the meanwhile, the medical section of Booke Mission was humming with activity. The Mission nurse and her African assistant started on the dot of 6 a.m.with a special meeting for all the outpatients waiting for treatment. The missionary or African evangelist would give a bright and animated message about God's love and salvation for all who repent of their sins and believe in Jesus as Saviour. Singing was a very noisy and joyful part of this half hour, and was greatly enjoyed by all. By half past six in the tropics the sun is already hot, and most folk would sit in the shade of trees nearby waiting for treatment. For really sick patients who needed 'bed' treatment we had a special village ¼ mile away, where they were attended by personal care and nursing. There would be 100 or more outpatients, who would walk back to their own villages, and maybe 10-20 inpatients in our hospital village. So a very busy day six days each week was the nurses' job. Often there were also maternity cases, and antenatal clinics whenever needed. Once a week leprosy patients came in for their injections or supply of medicines.

Often there were emergencies, such as leopard wounds or

snake-bites, broken bones or sudden collapse. All these had to be seen to, day or night, by the busy nurse. The medical work was exacting and exhausting—but well worthwhile.

The Bible School lectures were from 9.30-12.30 when several of the missionaries fitted in Bible lectures, evangelism, preaching, etc. The afternoons were spent in actually visiting villages and preaching to anyone ready to listen! This was excellent practice for our students, and rewarding. An early evening fireside meeting with lots of hymn singing in Lingala was a refreshing and stimulating finish to a hot and busy day!

And what about mothers who had small children to look after? Often missionary mothers were also school teachers and/or nurses, and had to fit in their work wherever possible. I was very fortunate in having a great helper in a dear elderly missionary—"Aunty Ko"—who never learned the African or French language, but was an "intercessor" and help for families. This was her role in life, and she was an amazing woman, full of love and faith. Her real name was Mary Kolachny. She started as a Czechoslovakian refugee to the U.S.A. Her parents were often drunk and very quarrelsome. She was converted wonderfully in the U.S.A. as a young teenager, and consequently cast out of her home and family by her irate parents. But Christians fostered her, and she eventually became a missionary to Congo—and so we inherited an amazing missionary helper!

Whatever time of day or night I had to go to attend an emergency in the hospital—accident or midwifery case (I was Booke Mission nurse)—"Aunty Ko" would always be available to watch the children and the baby! She would be responsible for the children for however long it had to be, one, two, or three hours, until I gave the 'all clear' for return to normal. Later she taught our children in her little school (in English, of course) and she was an excellent teacher and disciplinarian!

Aunty Ko was a great encourager,—but she did not shrink from reproving us if necessary. I remember on one occasion she had received an inner assurance that God would supply her need of a dressing gown and slippers. Now it so happened I had both in my wardrobe to spare and had more than once sensed that God was instructing me to pass them on to Aunty Ko, but I had not acted on that inner prompting. One day, Aunty Ko shared with me her puzzlement,

"You know, Joy, God has told me that He has a gown and slippers for me, but they still have not come. Something is not right." She had not "aimed" the comments at me, but I knew immediately that I was the one.

"The gown and the slippers that God has for you are in my wardrobe," I confessed. "For some time now God has been prompting me to give them to you, but I kept putting it off and making excuses. But I know they are for you. Here, let me get them." I felt no regret in passing them on, rather a sense of joy that my disobedience had changed to obedience. That incident marked my life, and ever since I have sought to obey God promptly when He tells me to do something or pass something on to someone else. Aunty Ko was God's instrument to teach me that lesson,—and others! More than once she had cause to reprimand me sharply for attitudes or words that were not honouring to God. But she never did it in a way which wounded or caused resentment. She lived close to God and sought to draw me nearer to Him. She was a true friend indeed.

I owe a great debt to dear Aunty Ko, whom I loved very dearly. Our four boys respected her and responded warmly to her remarkable influence. She was always determined that she would go straight to heaven from Booke and that is exactly what happened. She died and was buried by Colin and me in the jungle there at Booke in 1959. Praise God for Aunty Ko's remarkable influence on all of us missionaries and our children. She spent many African nights in prayer for each of us and our work. Only eternity will reveal just what her faith and prayer achieved.

7

Baby in a Box

One of the most testing times of our eventful life in "Congo" was when we had to make long journeys to our newest accredited hospital to have the attention and care of a qualified doctor.

The Belgian authorities insisted that all expatriate ladies must have their confinements in *bona fide* hospitals, and they would give financial assistance for this. So, when we knew that our third baby was on the way, we prayed for definite guidance: as to whether we should go to the Government hospital at Lodja, 280 miles away, or the American Mission 380 miles away. We knew Lodja Hospital had an excellent Belgian obstetrician/physician, and we could leave our two little boys, Colin (4) and Malcolm (2) with missionary "aunties" Grace and Marjorie *en route* at Loto, only 80 miles away from our mission.

All was arranged and we prepared the Chevrolet 1¼ ton truck for the journey via Loto mission. The two children were excited about the journey! "Never a dull moment" could describe that eventful five weeks away from our base at Booke mission! We spent several days at Loto resting and relaxing and settling Colin and Malcolm happily with their guardians, then set off for the remaining 200-mile stretch. On such occasions I always took my fully equipped midwifery bag—just in case we couldn't reach the hospital in time. Incidentally, not once in my four pregnancies did I have antenatal care or tests—distances were far too great for such things! So, on we lumbered in the heavy "Chev" truck, with equipment, food, and a small group of African helpers.

All went well, until we reached one bridge made of planks held down by forest creepers and rusty nails. It creaked ominously as we mounted it!—"What will this be like in two weeks time when we return?" we said to each other. Holding our breath as we could hear some of the trusses snapping and boards shifting under the wheels, we drove over safely to the other side. One plank dislodged and fell into the river below. Thanking God for safe travel so far, we sped on and on, eventually reaching an American mission station and a welcome from the kind lady missionary—"Please stay the night—you look worn out!" We insisted on just resting and having a quick break, because I was decidedly uncomfortable. The awful jogging over very rough roads was exhausting and disturbing. I was apprehensive. We did stop for a short rest, but I went into the guest room and fell on my knees—"Oh, Lord, please help me, I'm scared because things have started. Please help us to reach the doctor in time. Give me courage. Give me a word from yourself!" Opening my Bible, my eyes fell on the words in Psalm 50.15—"Call upon ME in the day of trouble; *I will deliver thee* and thou shalt glorify ME"! "Praise the Lord," I cried, and Colin and I felt reassured and upheld, and got back in the "Chevy" and rumbled on the five miles further to the hospital. It was getting dark now and what a relief to see the lights in the hospital windows. We staggered to the main entrance, knowing that I was in labour and that it couldn't be very long now. The nurse who came to the door looked horror-stricken—"Oh, the doctor has just gone up north in his Vanette to attend to an emergency 50 miles away! Do come in. We'll get everything ready now." The nurse and Colin had to attend to my care, and after midnight 30th December, a lovely baby boy was born.

Ten hours later, arriving back from his journey, the doctor breezed in and exclaimed "So you've all arrived!" But at that very moment Colin was overcome with violent vomiting and diarrhoea and collapsed on the nearby bed. The alarmed doctor examined him and ordered bed and specialised treatment and careful nursing, because the diagnosis was amoebic dysentery (with grave danger of an amoebic liver abscess following). Treatment had to begin at once and regularly through the following night. The doctor said he had all the drugs on hand, but Madame (i.e., myself), being a qualified nurse, would do all the nursing! So I had a two day old baby to attend to and a very sick husband. How we praised God for His amazing intervention. Surely He "delivered" us in our time of trouble by bringing us just in time for the right treatment to be administered. Had we remained at our mission we would have had no doctor and no suitable drugs. God helped us through that time of crisis in ways which we had not imagined. Baby Gordon was well looked after and mother and father survived with the doctor's help and certainly with the Lord's overwhelming love and care.

Two weeks later we were ready to leave for home in the Chevrolet truck with our tiny baby, and called in at the American Mission, five miles away, for fellowship and nourishment. Our kind and hospitable lady friend gave us a large carton box beautifully padded with soft material and tiny mattress as a "crib for the li'l' baby Gordon." (Something she always liked to supply for missionaries with new babies!) Bless her heart, little did she know how useful that crib would be.

We set off on our nearly 200 mile return journey, longing for our meeting up with Colin and Malcolm to show them baby Gordon,—hopefully that evening. Lumbering on, mile after mile of bumpy roads and jungle tracks, we looked apprehensively at the blackening sky. Soon we were splashing through torrential rain, with thunder and lightning making progress more difficult. But baby Gordon was safe and comfortable in his "cardboard crib" on Mother's lap. Suddenly the truck slithered to a standstill in deep mud—red and slippery right on the brink of the swollen river—water rushing fast down the valley with branches and debris flowing past. NO bridge at all—every plank washed away!

We gasped and looked in horror at the swirling water! What next? Just then two Africans appeared wet and dripping with large leafy "umbrellas" over their heads. "The bridge has been washed away (yes, we had noticed!) but the Government official is camped two miles across the other side and will come to meet you on that bank." They called a message over the river, and in the meantime felled a large tree right across from bank to bank. An African carefully hoisted the "cardboard crib" with baby Gordon tied in and placed it on his head and then proceeded to balance across the log bridge until he stepped off on the other side. It looked so easy for him, but next it was our turn. We must have looked like first-time tightrope walkers; the "rope" was thick enough, but it was slippery with the rain, and underneath was the fast-flowing water! What relief when we arrived wet and trembling on the other side!

The Belgian official arrived in his truck and apologised for the inconvenience! We were taken to his camp where his African wife and baby kindly vacated their bed on the floor for me and my baby, and we slept there that night. Our generous hosts gave us coffee and bread in the morning and borrowed two bicycles for us to cycle the remaining 35 miles to Loto mission. Our precious baby was placed in the box and tied on to the back on my bike, and the box protected from the rain with large forest leaves. And so, eventually, we cycled into Loto on the two bikes, with our baby happily asleep in a cardboard box!

The story was soon told, and we had to stay at the mission

for ten days until the bridge was completed, and Colin was able to return the bikes and collect the Chevrolet from the jungle. "Never a dull moment, indeed", but what a lot we praised God for! Our children were safe and well and so glad to welcome baby Gordon, none the worse for his first exciting adventure in Africa. Colin was able to rest and recuperate and complete his treatment. God had indeed delivered us from many dangers and had brought us safely through, and together we gave Him all the glory and praise!

8

Tears and Triumphs of Medical Work

Much of my time in Congo was allocated to midwifery, and I was personally responsible for delivering 104 Congolese babies. Sadly, five of these were stillborn. One dark evening at Booke we heard the shuffle of many running feet and agitated voices coming down the path towards our house. Going quickly to the door we saw two perspiring men carrying a hammock slung to a pole. In the hammock was a very sick patient, chilled and feverish—a young woman in advanced labour. On examination we realised that she must be taken immediately to hospital (80 miles through the jungle!) because she needed to have a caesarian operation to save her life.

Hastily we prepared a mattress on the floor of our pick-up and set off late in the night with patient lying on the mattress, and young husband and mother next to her on the floor. The journey would be long, bumpy, and tedious, and we prayed as we drove through the night for a safe and uneventful journey—for there was a big river with a pontoon which had to be negotiated en route! We hastened on to Kole hospital, and eventually put the case into the doctor's care.

The woman was immediately taken to the operating table. The baby was already dead, so the doctor told the husband that he would operate and remove the little dead child. He also warned the husband that there was little hope of saving the young mother's life. The relations argued that an operation would not be acceptable, and while they argued, the girl on the operating table collapsed and died. The relations still insisted that the dead baby must not be removed from its mother's body. So a very sad group of us packed into the pick-up with mourning relatives and dead mother and child, to return over the pontoon and back to Enga village to break this tragic news to the waiting relatives.

As we drove into the village, people swarmed around the truck, and as soon as they realized the truth an ear-splitting wail went up. They grabbed the corpse and rushed into the centre of the village, wailing and shrieking in a frenzy of anguish and grief. Amazingly quickly they wrapped the corpse into a long mat, and a shallow grave was prepared, and within minutes the body was covered over with earth and leaves. All this haste was because of the strong superstitions of the people that a corpse of "mother and child" was a great danger because of the evil spirits—and troubles and reprisals would come!

Then, suddenly, the weeping husband commanded everyone to sit down.

"The missionary will tell us all how we must all prepare for death, for we never know when death will catch up with us! LISTEN all of you!"

There was a deep and solemn hush as this large group of mourners listened to the message of God's salvation, and as the sun rose upon us all, so several villagers expressed a desire to believe in this great salvation! Tears turned to joy as several people really grasped the meaning of new life in Christ. Before we left for home, the village chief and the young husband asked us to send them an evangelist to teach them the way of the Lord. One of our Bible School students was sent to Enga and a lovely little church was built for regular worship and teaching.

Out of sadness—joy
out of tears—triumph!
out of death—LIFE!

I remember well another young woman who was in prolonged labour. I was anxious because there had been no progress. Once again we prepared the pick-up for the long drive to the doctor for a caesarian operation. We were relieved when we got to the pontoon crossing just 5 kms short of the hospital. We would soon be able to put the woman into the care of the surgeon. Suddenly things started happening in the back of the pick-up, and soon, there he was,—a beautiful 8lb baby boy! Shouts of joy and exclamations of delight! We drove the short remaining distance, showed mother and baby to the doctor, and drove all the way home again for a jubilant welcome at the woman's village.

In Africa we had to get used to the unexpected happening, and we learned to trust God for what was beyond our control. I recall vividly once when Colin and I travelled on an OTRACO steamboat up the Congo River. To our consternation we discovered that the steamer had taken an unscheduled turn up a tributary. The captain of the ship reassured us that it was only a temporary diversion, and that we would be back down the tributary to rejoin the Congo River in a day or two. Mooring overnight beside a remote riverside mission, we were welcomed by a very anxious missionary whose wife was dangerously ill with double pneumonia. He was overjoyed to hear I was trained nurse, and from that moment I was busy nursing her. We let the boat go back downstream without us, knowing that God had sent us here to minister to His servants. We stayed a whole week, catching the following boat downstream. The lady was nursed back to good health and we all had several days of happy fellowship together, culminating in a service of thanksgiving for her restoration.

The regular medical work at Booke kept us very busy from the 6.30 a.m. service until midday. Patients were examined and treated. Diseases were many and varied: leprosy, malaria, gonorrhoea and syphilis, skin infections of all sorts, disentery, typhoid, and microfilaria. Measles was a killer for small children, and so were small-pox and pneumonia. I remember some cases of yaws where the child's body was so covered with great open sores that it was difficult to find a clear patch of skin in which to put the injection.

In addition to the regular diseases, there were the wounds caused by animals and snakes. I remember one particularly tragic case. A hunter named Mpela, pushing his way through the undergrowth, caught his foot in the trip-wire of an elephant trap. He thereby released a heavily weighted spear suspended from a branch high above. In its downward rush it penetrated the skin of his back just behind his head and passed down the entire length of his back between the skin and the spine, emerging between his buttocks. He was brought into the dispensary with the 5-foot spear still where it was. We had to extract the spear as carefully as possible, then wash the wound out with warm saline solution. You can imagine the agony and fear the man must have been in. Much prayer was offered for poor Mpela's recovery, and God answered our prayer.

Mpela was profoundly grateful. He was as surprised as everyone else that he had survived. Everyone had been sure he would die. Mpela lived for several years at Booke, and heard the Gospel. It made a great impression on him, and we were delighted when one day it dawned on him that God loved *him* and that Jesus died for *him*. He became a true and eloquent witness to God's power to save and to heal.

9

Mother's Day

The missionary house-wife mother in Congo has multitudinous tasks and endless interruptions. Many are the varied calls upon her time from morning to night. She deals with a frequently changing staff of African helpers, all of whom needed to be initiated into the strange ways that we wanted things done. Here then is a typical day in my life in Congo.

The first streaks of dawn grow in the east, and the trees begin to emerge from the black of night into the early morning bluey haze, as I seek a time alone with the Lord. The only sounds that break the cool stillness are the incessant buzz of insects in the tropical forest, and the intermittent crowing of roosters.

Later, as the sun peeps over the horizon of treetops, peace and quiet give place to noise and bustle and activity. By 6 a.m. the children are up, and I feed the baby, make beds, tidy up, etc. Then household tasks and instructions are allotted to the African helpers, while I try to put away last night's laundry, only to be called away urgently by the cook to solve some problem in the kitchen out-house. At the door are two women and children to sell sweet potatoes and onions, while others come to buy soap or salt (the nearest store of any size is 60 miles away!) I no sooner reach the house than another buyer comes for rice, but has not brought anything to carry it home in and expects me to furnish a tin for the rice. He also expects me to give him patches for his ragged shirt... "Are you not our mother?" he asks. "Don't you provide the needs of your children?"

The breakfast bell furnishes a good excuse to retreat into the house. After breakfast the missionaries meet for morning prayers. Then I literally dash from one task to another. I quickly mix up a pudding for dinner (as the cook has not yet mastered this art!), prepare the baby's feeds, attend to four or five more callers at the door, then go to bath and feed the baby. Outside I can hear hot arguing and shouting...whatever can it be?...The irate cook shouts across: "Mama, these wicked schoolboys are liars and deceivers! They're going off duty and still have one more turn of water to draw!" Shrieks from the house...one of the children has fallen and hurt his knee...medicines and bandages to the rescue. I attempt to tackle some machining, get one seam sewn and am called urgently away to buy bananas: "Mother, buy quickly! You see the rain is coming and I must get back to my village." But before going they must see the baby. "Oh, what a beautiful baby! Truly a fine baby! Now, what will you give us for admiring your child?" I flee for refuge with the gurgling infant, and fail to reappear. I pop the baby into the pram for his morning nap, and hasten to teach arithmetic in the school for an hour, then tackle some more sewing.

There's always plenty of sewing and mending, for I make all my own and the children's clothes, the nearest clothing shop being hundreds of miles away. But again an African appears: "Mother, make <u>me</u> a pair of shorts." I exclaim in anguish that it's quite impossible as I can hardly cope with the family's needs, let alone make others' things. Then more buyers and sellers appear; and when at last they've gone, I seek refuge at the organ, feeling rather distracted. "Peace, perfect peace" swells out volubly, but three notes are dead, so the effect is not so soothing! "Mama!..."—a man wants to buy salt, and (just after he is seen to) a woman wants some too,...etc. I seize the opportunity of a lull to play one more verse: "Peace, perfect peace, by thronging duties pressed. To do the will of Jesus, this is rest." It seems a paradox, but the truth of it steals over my heart, and courage and peace are renewed. And so the day goes on, until night falls and rest comes again, and the quietness of the night allows me to seek Him.

"Lord, nothing seems to have gone according to plan...

"I have had so many interruptions... people everywhere.

"Are we to deal patiently with their ceaseless affairs and endless requirements?"

And the Lord seems to reply tenderly: "Inasmuch as you have done it unto the least of these... you have done it to Me."

Thank You, Lord.

And together Colin and I go round the four small beds and kiss each precious little one lying peacefully slumbering and whisper: "Thank You for the love and laughter of these little ones ... Good night."

Often I used to feel perplexed and frustrated by the interruptions and unimportant happenings of the typical day, and can remember so well one Saturday afternoon being in the kitchen mixing up a cake for the weekend. I was feeling particularly jaded because all week I had really accomplished nothing in the way of "missionary work"—just the endless round of common tasks. I was indulging in a good grumble and grouse—"Lord I don't seem to have done any "spiritual" work lately—there are no opportunities to preach the Gospel in the kitchen!" Hardly had I breathed this "prayer" than I heard an insistent cough at the door, and moaned "Oh! another interruption". But actually a dear distraught African woman was calling to me saying she was in great distress because she had had a bad nightmare in the night and was terrified. "God told me I must repent of my sins and become Christian at once! So I have come to do just that. It is urgent!"

While the cake was baking in the oven, Mpela and I sat in the kitchen together, and I was able to explain to her the Way of Salvation. She was absolutely ready to give her life to the Saviour, and we finished our little service with thanksgiving to God for His great love and forgiveness, peace and joy.

Mpela went back to her village with new faith and assurance—and I praised God for so marvellous an answer to a Mother's prayer! Also I felt reproved by the Lord. His will is simply that we should be available for Him to use as He wishes; to be His hands serving the needs of others, and to be His mouth sharing the good news of His love with those who do not know Him.

10

God's Amazing Provision

In the midst of a very busy and exhausting programme on the Booke Mission Station, and while our three boys were still away at Sakeji School, I suddenly realised that I was expecting a fourth baby. The idea appalled me and I felt rebellious. How could I cope with another baby? We had decided that our family was complete—and now!

My weary heart reacted badly. I felt angry. Colin was to blame. Colin was asking too much. I had been foolish. Disgruntled and discouraged, I felt like grumbling and grousing—all joy had disappeared! My poor husband wondered what all the fuss was about!

My dear colleague Aunty Ko noticed how miserable I was. That was one of the hard things on a confined mission station! Nothing kept hidden for long—and everybody knew that there was something wrong! Aunty Ko, shrewdly discerning as ever, exclaimed that there was something radically wrong—I was so snappy and glum! It all came out in a rush,

"I'm expecting another baby, and I am not pleased. Colin my husband is overworked and not well; I am harassed and burdened, and I don't want this baby. I can't cope!"

You will remember that Aunty Ko was one for straight talking. She sat down with me and declared, "Joy, you are embittered and angry. Your attitude is not right. You must repent and instead say "Thank you" to God for this new life coming to us."

"It's all very well for you!" I retorted. "You don't understand. You are single and have no family worries."

However, God began working in my rebellious heart, especially when dear Aunty Ko declared that the new baby within me could be seriously affected by my attitude and lack of acceptance—"You must get this serious matter right with God!" she concluded.

I had not told anybody else about this (except my husband) so I did go to the Lord about it and admitted I was angry, frustrated and rebellious,—but I really was sorry. "Please, Lord, give me a new attitude altogether! And please, Lord, I have nothing at all in the way of clothes for a new baby—everything has been given away two years ago to other expectant mothers. So please forgive and cleanse me from every wrong attitude, and prove to me Your forgiveness by supplying a complete layette—down to even safety pins!!" A great burden fell off my shoulders, and I had no doubt whatever God had forgiven and cleansed, and would supply me with everything for the new baby! From that moment I rejoiced that we were well on the way to having baby No.4. Whether girl or boy, this little one would be welcomed and well cared for. Praise God! I ran across the grass and told dear Aunty Ko that all was well—I was now rejoicing!

Less that two weeks passed and the mail-bag arrived with a letter from my mother, 3500 miles away in South Africa, which I eagerly opened, because it was always so lovely to hear from "home". She told me an extraordinary story about a young Christian woman who had just left four big parcels of baby clothes—a complete layette, in fact—to be given to any missionary up in Congo who was expecting a baby! Amazingly, this woman had been advised by her doctor to get rid of *everything* which was reminding her of the tragic "still-birth" of the baby they had just lost. She was on the verge of a nervous breakdown because she was constantly looking at and grieving over those baby clothes and little things she had prepared. She was very anxious to know if I knew of anyone who was expecting a baby! The doctor told her she must have a good holiday, and deliberately look forward to next year, when she could plan for another child.

All this complete layette, even to a card of lovely new safety pins and talcum powder, came in four big parcels to Booke Mission. I *was* the next expectant mother! My eyes filled with tears, my heart was humbled and also gladdened, as Colin and I opened these four parcels and found a literal answer to prayer and abundant supply of *every* need for my new baby. Not a thing missing, every detail answered—even down to safety pins!! Fantastic! "My God shall supply all your needs."

Even my mother had not been told that I was expecting another baby! Marvellous! We were amazed at how speedily God works when we face up to our wrong attitude, confess, and truly repent. He then loves to work miracles for us.

I must hasten to add that we followed up the case of the dear lady who gave up her complete layette. God gave her renewed health, and the following year she did have her heart's desire fulfilled, and had the joy of gathering a complete wardrobe of baby clothes for her new treasure.

I had a happy and very busy pregnancy and eventually Colin and I went back to Lodja, 280 miles away (where Gordon had been born four years earlier), for the arrival of our fourth child. This time the doctor was available and present, and we soon went on our way rejoicing, with baby David in top form. During that pregnancy, as in all the other three, we had claimed afresh God's wonderful promise—"He has blessed your children *within* you." (Psalm 147.13)

On our arrival back with the new baby we dedicated him to the Lord in the church with all our Africans present—Christians and non-Christians—claiming again for this NEW

LIFE the promise—"*All your children* shall be taught by the Lord, and great shall be the peace of your children." (Isaiah 54.13). And God did bless them all.

To me, as I look back on the experiences gained, I realise how wonderful is God's wisdom and patience and understanding. He worked out His purposes in the lives of two young mothers—both having gone through serious crises in their lives, both having learned valuable lessons. Truly God's ways are wonderful—His love and compassion beyond our expectations.

11

The Great Escape

June 1960 was a momentous time for the Belgian Congo, when that huge country was granted independence; a general revolt by the Congolese army took place and there was great unrest and suspicion. The Congolese insisted that their Belgian "oppressors" should quit the country at once and leave it to them. So there was a mass exodus of Belgian women and children who were airlifted to their homeland; the men remained behind to clear up and salvage as much as they could of their property and possessions. They were supported by a handful of loyal Congolese, who promised to help them get away to safety.

Our Mission, the African Evangelistic Band (based in South Africa), consisted of four mission stations spread over an area of 150 by 200 miles, so we were strongly advised by our Belgian friends to meet at Kole Mission in order to evacuate all 35 of us (including 16 children) the following Saturday. We were all much in prayer about this, for none of us wanted to leave the work in which we had been involved for so many years.

Colin and I went to visit Kokitale village for the weekend so as to give the impression that all was "normal", and not cause unrest among the local people. That Sunday was very precious, because we had a hallowed communion service with our dear African Christians. We were suddenly interrupted by a woman (who up until then had wanted nothing to do with God) rushing in to say she must *"right now"* confess her sins to God and trust in Jesus. There was a hush after this, and the woman was helped to faith in Christ. Then we sang praises to God for His salvation! Very soon after that, Colin and I continued on our journey to Kole to finalise arrangements with the government officials, agreeing that we would join their convoy of cars next Saturday with our seven roadworthy vehicles. But we had to agree to have an armed soldier in each car for our protection.

As we drove the 100 miles back to Booke Mission, we felt perplexed and sad. We did not like the idea of dashing non-stop through 400 miles of jungle with "arms at the ready!" But those were the conditions. A verse from Daniel 3.17 kept coming to us like a telegram—"Our God, whom we serve, is able to deliver us and He will deliver us."

Arriving back at midnight, we went straight to bed, exhausted and grateful. Morning prayers at 8 a.m.saw our group of six missionaries together, and we told them what we had to face—to leave Booke in two days' time and meet all our other missionaries together with seven vehicles at Kole for evacuation southwards via Luluabourg (Kananga) on Saturday. This news was a shock to everyone. We wondered how we could be ready in time.

Referring to the little book of Scripture readings "Daily Light" for that day, 12th July, we were amazed to see how the verses fitted our conditions! "My Presence shall go with you and I will give you rest" (Exodus 33.14). "Be strong and of good courage, fear not nor be afraid of them, for the Lord your God is with you wherever you go!" "The Lord goes before you… He will be with you… HE will not fail you… fear not, do not be dismayed." Imagine what assurance and comfort we had from these wonderful words! So all that day and the next we were packing up and preparing to make a quick and silent get-away. On the 13th I was called out into the yard, where the local witch doctor, seething with anger, was demanding that we missionaries should leave as soon as possible. "We never wanted you to come," he shouted, brandishing his double-edged spear in my face. One of our Christian men tried to pacify him by reminding him that the missionaries "came to help us with the Gospel and medical help and schools" – but our enemy plainly was glad to see us go.

That evening after dark our two evangelists came to us secretly and said there was a sinister atmosphere and that many of our enemies were hiding in the jungle waiting for an appropriate moment. They pleaded urgently with us, "Before the first cock crows, about 2.30 a.m., when there is a great silence, you should leave Booke."

We had prayer with these faithful friends and committed one another to God's safe keeping for them and for us. Colin managed to get two hours sound sleep in before our departure. But I sat in the office writing a full letter to my dear mother in South Africa – unable to relax until I had opened my heart to her on paper. There was that feeling that we might never make it – others had perished in their attempts to escape. So I wrote feverishly until suddenly I heard the dining room clock strike 12 midnight. With a sigh, I finished the long epistle.

Picking up "Daily Light" again on the new day (14th), I read "out of the abundance of the heart the mouth speaketh" (Matthew 10.34), and on the opposite page, "I trust I shall shortly SEE thee and *we shall speak* face to face." (3 John v.14) Undoubtedly God was speaking these words to ME – He understood everything I had said and thought. He was assuring me that I would soon speak face to face with Mother. With delight I tore the whole letter into shreds – Praise God!

Less than two hours afterwards we were boarding our two cars – and without further hesitation drove up the narrow road through the jungle surrounding our Mission Station with headlights piercing the African night and causing weird shadows to dance and lurch as we moved forward. We kept going, the while praying fervently that we would not meet any elephants on the road or that hostile locals would not block the road by felling trees across it. Without any incident we sped through the sleeping villages and lapped up the 100 mile stretch to Kole. By morning, other vehicles came lumbering in with the rest of our missionaries, and we were given the use of a large house to "camp in" to await the hour of our departure.

Some hours later a panting and perspiring evangelist Bosao Paul came rushing in on his bicycle—"I must tell you how wonderfully God allowed you to get away just in time in the morning at Booke. Your cars had only just disappeared into the darkness of the jungle when the hostile villagers, who had indeed been hiding in the forest, swooped in and ransacked the homes and hospital, looting and plundering everything. Even your refrigerator was smashed by a hatchet. Many of your possessions carried away! Thank God you all got away safely! I had to come and tell you!" So after a short rest, our faithful friend started his 100 miles ride back by bike. It had been a dangerous thing for him to come and tell us and then return. Praise God for His protection of our dear Christian friends, who did not suffer physical hardship, but carried on the work of God in spite of our sudden departure.

While there at Kole mission some Baluba soldiers came to "protect" us—but we felt more intimidated than helped! One huge fellow with 45 bullets round his waist and a big gun in his hand said we would be safe with him. But we prayed the more earnestly that God would keep these men from doing us bodily harm. They even confiscated our lanterns and torches for the night which left us absolutely helpless in pitch darkness!

The next day dawned and we knew this was the Saturday we agreed to meet the Belgian convoy at Kole State Post five miles away. All vehicles were checked and packed ready for the 400 mile dash to Luluabourg. We were feeling disturbed by the day's news that many white people were being molested, raped, and robbed—and there was growing unrest!

As we stood by our vehicles ready to go, someone shouted "Hey! There are two tiny airplanes zig-zagging towards us from the south. Look!" Sure enough, two little Cessnas were buzzing lower overhead, obviously having spotted us all standing round with seven vehicles ready to go! A note weighted down together with a pencil fell at our feet, on it the message: *"Do you want to be rescued? – If so, put out a sheet immediately!"* Do we want to be rescued?! Someone dashed into the house and grabbed a sheet. We held it out between four of us. Yes, please! By the time the two planes had landed on a nearby field, we were there to meet them. They were horrified that we were just about to leave for Luluabourg—"You can't go there! Impossible! There are airplanes and cars burning on the ground. Nothing can get away from Luluabourg!! You must abandon all hope of going there. We will come tomorrow and airlift all 35 of you—but only *two kilos of baggage each*. Leave everything! Your very lives are at stake!"

So we were all left at Kole for the night, our American friends returning to the base at Lodja to arrange for a Dakota to come and evacuate us all from there. As soon as their two planes left, my husband and I went by car the five miles to Kole Government Post to tell the officials that we would not be coming with them after all—only to find that they and their vehicles and armed escorts had left six hours before! They had been tipped off by friendly Congolese that if they didn't leave by midday they and their vehicles would be destroyed or taken over. So there wasn't a sign of anyone—all gone! We gasped! If those American pilots had not come, how and where would we have gone?

And just then we were handed a letter which had filtered through, in which was quoted an amazing verse (Psalm 34.7)

"The angel of the Lord encamps round about those that fear Him and delivers them". This letter had been written by our 17 year old son Colin as an encouragement to our faith! We needed courage and faith right then.

Another thing we discovered, to our horror, was that even if we had wanted to follow the convoy, to try and catch up with them would be impossible, because the pontoon over the Lukenyi River at Kole had been cut loose from its moorings, and so there was no way across. We looked in horror at the great river!

How we praised God for His miraculous intervention just in the nick of time! We slept fitfully that night, all sharing beds and rooms—and in the early morning, our American friends returned by Cessna plane to airlift us the 80 miles eastward over impenetrable forest to Lodja. By another miracle the American Dakota plane was caught just before it was going off to South America on another errand. We got this only because in our group of 35 missionaries there happened to be one American lady with an American passport—so all of us were granted the use of the American Ambassador's plane from Pretoria! This was a 12-seater luxury plane, usually used for V.I.P's , but all seats were removed and we managed to squeeze all 35 of us plus five extra passengers and the pilot! And so, eventually, we were airborne—heavily laden and uncomfortable, wedged together on the floor of the plane, but on our way! As I looked tearfully down on our beloved African jungle, feeling very sad that we had to leave in such a way, the verse came forcibly to mind—Jesus' words to his disciples "I go to prepare a place for you." If He so plans for us for eternity, then surely He has us in His heart for our life here on earth, too. It gave us great comfort and assurance for the future.

And so we flew on southwards via Kamina, the Rhodesias (now Zambia and Zimbabwe) and eventually to Johannesburg in South Africa. Friends were there to meet us with warm clothing and hot drinks for we were all suffering from shock—airlifted from hot tropical jungles to a bitterly cold airport with snow on the ground. We were all given meals and a warm welcome for several days in the Johannesburg area, and later helped to get to our various destinations.

Colin and I eventually arrived in Fish Hoek, near Cape Town. My mother and I hugged each other, crying and laughing together. We told of the experiences of 13th and 14th July, and God's promises to us. She pointed to a calendar clipping which was pinned to a kitchen curtain.

"Joy," my mother exclaimed, "You must take that down and read it!" The clipping was dated July 14th, 1960,—*"The salvation of the righteous is of the Lord—He is their strength in time of trouble. And the Lord shall help them and deliver them; He shall deliver them from the wicked because they trust in Him"—(Psalm 37. 39,40)* This was God's promise to Mother and her friend during their uncertainty and anxiety.

Then she told us how on July 13th in the evening she had felt so burdened for our safety in Congo that she called in a neighbour and they prayed together in the kitchen for several hours, indeed until the clock struck midnight, and Mother's friend exclaimed, "We must start praising God for His deliverance!"

My poor mother said. "I can't feel any assurance yet. But let's look at the calendar for this new day (14th). Listen to this!" And she read those amazing words, and faith sprang into her heart. This was God's promise of what He was doing right NOW! So in faith she pinned the paper on the curtain, saying joyfully, "Let Joy *herself* take that down when they come and join us." Praise God! We laughed and cried together—and, of course, had several cups of tea!

Then Colin read a favourite passage, Psalm 40.1-3: *"I waited patiently for the Lord—He heard my cry. He brought me* <u>*UP*</u> *(airplanes!)—set my feet upon a rock—and established my goings. And He has put a new song in my heart, even praise to our God. Many shall see it and fear, and shall trust in the Lord."*

This last promise from the Bible was literally fulfilled, for we were able to tell this story all over the country, and many were blessed and their faith strengthened by God's wonderful dealings with us.

When we had to abandon everything there at Kole, even Bibles were too heavy to take. I tore out very carefully several pages of our "Daily Light" (10th to 20th July inclusive) and kept them safely on my person until later when I was able to sew the pages together. In those dark hours of extremity and danger, the Word of God became very precious. At the end we were able to praise God together for His promises: "This is the Lord's doing. It is marvellous in our eyes!" Psalm 118.23.

12

ENCOUNTER WITH THE LION

Our years in Congo provided us with a sense of adventure which has stayed with us long after we had to leave the work in that land. One exciting incident Colin and I had was during a return visit to South Africa where my mother and various other relatives lived. What transpired on that occasion was rather too adventurous even for us. Here's what happened. Over the years, Colin and I were asked to tell the story many times. We would usually tell the story between us, taking turns. The story was even printed in leaflet form and a 78rpm record made of our shared story. So that is how it is told here, with Colin starting off.

"We've come," I said, still rather breathless.

"Who are you?" demanded the uniformed Game Warden, as he turned round and looked at us, "Where have you come from?"

"From out there," I said, nodding vaguely towards the darkness.

"How did you get in here?"

I hesitated, knowing the strict laws of the Game Reserve; "...er, we walked."

"You what?!" exploded the Warden, and with the explosion others, staff and visitors at the Camp, turned round to look at us. We must have looked a sorry sight as we stood there, hot, dusty, dirty, bedraggled. Whether it was the sight of us or whether it was our next remark I don't know, but soon they began gathering around us in some amazement.

"We walked in these last three miles."

Questions began to flow thick and fast: what had happened? where had we come from? why had we done it?—and so on. Then one of them, more observant than the others, said: "Wait a minute. Sit down here and drink this." We obeyed and after a while began to feel rather more coherent and lucid. "Now," they said, "tell us what happened."

We told them.

Joy (my wife) and I were on a return visit to our beloved Africa, and an understanding and generous-minded friend had lent us her car for the whole of the time we were in that eastern part of the Transvaal. This little car had a low mileage reading, and it went splendidly as we soon discovered bowling along the great South African highways. We were not all that far from the Kruger National Park and we could not resist the temptation to go and spend a few days back in the Game reserve. "Won't it be grand to be back there again!" we said to each other, and I pressed the accelerator lower still in my excitement.

We arrived at the entrance to the Game Reserve only to find the gates all barred and bolted. Lunch hour, of course. We must wait until 2.15. We needn't have hurried quite so much. Impatiently we waited, with all the sights, sounds and smells of that part of Africa making the delay the more intolerable. Then at last we were in.

"Where will you be tonight? Which camp inside the reserve will you be staying at?" asked the official at the gate, "I must let them know so that they can be ready for you."

We told him.

"Yes, you ought to be able to do that easily in the time, but remember you must be in there before 6 o'clock. The Camp closes then and everyone must report in before they lock the gates for the night."

"Yes, we'll be there all right" we promised—and we were off. It was thrilling to be back in the great Game Reserve once again, and we searched the thick underbrush hopefully as we drove slowly along the dusty road.

Thinking we saw the form of some animal among the bushes, we pulled up. False alarm. Just the contorted branches deceiving us. But what was more disconcerting was that suddenly for some reason or other the engine, which had always started so easily, now remained sullen and silent. I tried everything I knew. The engine was defiant.

"There's nothing for it," I said, "We'll have to push it."

"We can't," said Joy, "you remember the lecture the man at the entrance gate gave us, that in no circumstances must we get out of the car? They're frightfully strict about it, you know."

This brought renewed efforts with the starter, but—no response. Laws or no laws we must do something. We clambered out of the car, gave it a hearty push, engaged the gear and we were off once more.

Soon it began stopping of its own accord—animals or no animals—and every time the starter proved utterly dead. Not supposed to leave the car, we knew, but we must just look in the boot. It was empty: no crank, no tools, nothing. So more pushing; more starting on hills; but all the time it was clear the engine even when it was running had less and less power. Down-hills were welcomed with cheers; up-hills with groans. I don't think there were many animals about, but we were in no mood to spend our time looking at them in any case for we were beginning to realise that we couldn't possibly reach the camp before it closed. This was serious, especially as we reflected on the many dangerous animals there were everywhere in the Reserve, and especially as once again the car, no longer heeding any exhortation on starter or accelerator, came to a sickening standstill.

By this time, with dusk drawing in, we cast discretion to

the winds and were in and out of the car every few minutes, pushing, coaxing, perspiring... till at last even these efforts proved fruitless. Nothing would produce the faintest glimmer of response in that sulky, stubborn engine. Not an inch further would it go. Joy and I debated: what should we do? It was now just about dark. Either we lock ourselves in the car and spend the night there amongst the animals, or we leave the car and walk in to the Camp. We reckoned we must still be about three miles from the Camp and the prospect of walking those three miles in the dark through a region we knew was inhabited by elephants, lions and other animals cast something of a shiver down our spines. Joy, of course, being a woman was entitled to such shivers; but I, a big bold male, should have no truck with such weaknesses. All the same, it was I who suggested rather lamely that perhaps after all we had better spend the night in the car. It was a half-hearted suggestion though, for both Joy and I had seen in the Congo the mess an angered elephant can make of a car. We had seen quite a large American car turned over on its side by one of these great monsters: how much more easily could it do that and much more besides to our poor little Escort? With that Congo picture vivid in our minds, "Come on," we said, "let's walk."

We set off. I can't say altogether courageously. It was now almost dark; we were already pretty exhausted with the tremendous heat of the afternoon and the much pushing. We did not appear a particularly noble couple as we set forth on our three mile walk: I gripping my precious briefcase in one hand and a small pocket torch in the other. Soon after we left the shelter of the car there was a roar, which was followed be a stampede on the part of a herd of zebra, and some more of those spinal shivers on our part. If there had been a dearth of animals in the afternoon, there were plenty of them all around now. Some we could see, many more we could smell and hear. "Let's keep going," we exhorted each other, but not with much enthusiasm or conviction in our voices.

By this time it was getting dark. Were we right in calculating the distance to the Camp as being only three miles? We thought so. Supposing we had miscalculated; supposing it were still some five miles to go. Was it sense to go on? Should we not rather go back even yet to the car and spend the night there? Some rather unpleasant noises behind us put this idea out of our heads. We went on. A hyena howled over to our right, bushes suddenly rustled unnaturally by the side of the path, then there was a rush of some animal over there. We went on, but this time we were holding each other's hand in a courage-inducing grip. "Can't be much further," we told each other, but it was on and on we went in the gathering darkness.

(Now I, Joy, take up the story)

Then at last we came on a stone pillar that assured us that the Tourist Camp was only 0.8 miles away, and this put a new spring into our lagging steps. Suddenly we froze. Just ahead of us our road crested a small hill, and there against the evening sky was the shape of a lioness gazing down on us intently and moving its long tail slowly from side to side. In spite of the intense heat we felt cold with fear, and we whispered—"What shall we do! We can't go back—the only way is forward." Hoping and praying she would move off and let us pass, we walked on talking to each other loudly so as to make her think we hadn't noticed!! Colin quoted a verse in Hebrews which said "through faith they stopped the mouths of lions"—and we fervently prayed that God would do just that for us. Steadily we walked on towards this beautiful (and terrifying) animal, fixing our eyes on her steady gaze. Now she was only 10 feet away to our right. She would not budge. Still talking and walking steadily forward, we began going down the slope and, looking furtively back, we saw she was still standing there. Heaving sighs of relief and fatigue we stumbled on—and just then caught sight of lights from the Tourist Camp. Safety at last!

Our intense relief turned to dismay and disbelief as we saw that the enormous Main Gate was bolted and barred. There was no sentry to let us in. Some way further in there was the sound of loud disco music. A 10ft high barricade stood before us, designed, ironically, to ensure the safety of all tourists. There was nothing for it but to scale this barrier. Somehow we clambered up and over, I first, then Colin, and half jumped, half fell onto the sandy ground on the inner side of the fence. Helping each other up and on we eventually reached Reception area and were met by the Game Warden and two or three others. Weary and footsore we exclaimed "We've come!" – and it was at that point that the conversation took place which started this chapter.

They must have been aware of our mental and physical exhaustion, for very soon they packed us off to bed, with borrowed clothing and toothbrushes (our things were still in the car!) and upon a last order from the Manager we were given a strong sedative to ensure we slept.

We were awakened by an African waiter giving us a tray of morning tea and a letter from the Game Warden. "So very sorry about last night's experience. Please will you both have breakfast with us at 8.30 a.m...."

The previous night there had been a big supper and dance, with lots of loud music and plenty of drink. The Warden and his wife took the evening off and joined in all the revelry, having completely overlooked the fact that two tourists and their Fiesta car had not arrived. Then, at about 9pm, two very exhausted guests arrived – obviously really done in! Having heard our story, they quickly packed us off to bed. No more dancing! They returned home to their house really worried. "You know, these people could report our negligence to the authorities! We should have gone out searching for them and their car, but they had to abandon it 3 miles out in the bush, and walk, and then scale the 10ft fence. How on earth did they manage that? Incredible!" First thing in the morning decided that they must invite us to breakfast and get in a strong apology! So that's how Colin and I found ourselves in the Game Warden's residence for a good breakfast.

Once again they asked us where we came from and who we were, and we soon told them we were Christian missionaries revisiting South Africa, that we had had all manner of dangerous encounters in Congo, but never such an experience as last night! We also added that the greatest thrill in our lives as missionaries was to see the amazing transformation that Jesus Christ has made in people. Through medical, educational and evangelical work we were helping to build the Church of Christ in darkest Africa. Our friends listened intently, and the whole thing became emotional, because they both said "We once knew what it was to be keen Christians, belonging to a live church, but the love of money and "living it up" made us turn our backs on it all. But last night we realised how futile and worthless it all is — no lasting satisfaction and no real joy. We want God to forgive us. And please will you, too, and we will return to our real faith in Jesus our Saviour. There are great opportunities in this place to serve God. If only we hadn't wasted these years! Will you please pray for us both?"

Of course we were amazed and overjoyed at this extraordinary turn of events and we did together pray and praise the Lord for His wonderful love and patience with us, His wayward children. And Colin opened his little pocket New Testament to 2 Timothy 4.17 & 18. "Notwithstanding, the Lord stood by me — and I was delivered from the mouth of the lion! And the Lord shall deliver me (us!) from every evil work, and will preserve us unto His Heavenly Kingdom, to whom be glory for ever and ever — AMEN." Our friends were humbled and joyous — all at once. We rejoiced together in God's great forgiveness and cleansing.

After breakfast the Warden took us in his powerful four

wheel drive LandRover to retrieve the Ford Escort. It was towed over thirty miles to a town outside the Reserve and put into a reputable garage for servicing (at the Warden's expense!) and we were served a lovely meal in an air-conditioned hotel.

Three hours later we all went on our way rejoicing—our new friend to his home in the Game Reserve, and we to our next assignment.

Colin & Joy, 1989

13

When one Door Closes—Another Opens

When Colin and I arrived back in England from Congo in 1961, we had it in mind to return to a different type of missionary work in Africa, but it did not work out. What we really needed was a work in England, so that we could have a home-base for our four sons who all had to have further education.

One day in 1962, Colin was approached by the Nepal Evangelistic Band (now known as INF) to consider an appointment as General Secretary, representing the work in Nepal at the home (UK) end. At first the idea did not appeal to us, since we were very Africa-orientated, and we had no knowledge of Nepal or its people. However, we prayed much about it and asked God to guide us and, if this was His will, to make us willing. One morning, reading John chapter 10, I was suddenly arrested by verse 16:—"other sheep I have which are not of this fold. Them also I must bring, and there shall be one fold and one shepherd." Being reminded of God's loving concern for people in all parts of the world prompted us to respond to this challenge of the work in Nepal.

A wonderful seal of affirmation came shortly after. Funds were very low in the NEB at that time, so the Mission could only pay for Colin alone to travel to Nepal to acquaint himself with the work there. I keenly wanted to accompany Colin so that I could be of greater assistance to him in the work and also bring a woman's ear to the many lady missionaries working in Nepal. But if I wished to go, £500 would be needed to cover my expenses. We were already booked for some meetings in Devon and Cornwall, and in the meantime we committed this need to the Lord.

During our travels in the West Country, we called in for coffee at the home of Mrs. C. In the course of conversation she suddenly said, "Last night in a dream, God told me to give Joy a cheque for £500!" She went on to ask if we had any special needs or whether we had been praying for such a sum. We were overwhelmed at this amazing answer to prayer,—and so was she, that she had got her instructions right! We spent some time right then, rejoicing together in prayer for this double confirmation that God wanted us both to go the Nepal.

A few weeks later we did both travel to Nepal, praying that God would help us adjust quickly to a land so different from Congo. We prayed that we would be able to minister to the missionaries, and get clear insights into the needs of the work there. It soon became evident that it was as well that we both went because most of the missionaries at that time were single women, and much better visited by a couple. While in Nepal for five weeks, I prayed that God would give me a special role alongside Colin. As we visited and talked with the missionaries out there, I could not help but notice that certain buildings were urgently needed,—for example, a house suitable for 2 single lady missionaries, and a kitchen and outhouse for the leprosarium. These would cost £800 each to build. Was this something I could help bring about?

As soon as we were back in England, I started special sales to supply these urgent needs. These "Sale and Gift" days attracted friends and church members who not only came to purchase articles, but also donated items which we then priced and displayed. All proceeds went to the designated project. It was a thrill when the first sales brought in the £800 for the nurses' bungalow in Nepal, and an even greater thrill when, before long, the bungalow was actually built and occupied. Then followed a kitchen for the leprosarium.

After that initial start, there were at least 2 sales a year in our home. People would bring items at any time and they would be stored in the loft in our home in Ewell: clothing (including a wedding dress!), small cookers, crockery and cutlery, costume jewellery, kitchen ware, books, glassware, toys, tools, cakes and preserves, etc. When the loft started to get congested, we would announce another Sale and Gift Day for an appropriate project. Often the projects would relate to some need in Nepal, but there were all sorts of other worthy causes in other parts of the world: a student home in a Bible School in Congo, bicycles for evangelists, protective paint for Bible College roofs, funding for young people on short-term mission overseas, typewriters for national Bible School teachers, and many other projects. We lost count just how many of these special sales we held during the years that Colin and I were with the INF. They continued in the years following Colin's retirement from the Mission in 1978, and even after Colin's death in 1989, I have held others on a smaller scale.

The other day I came across some diary jottings relating to one of the sales back in 1986, and I reproduce some of it here to give an idea of what went into these sales:

– *Mid-April: the attic is becoming uncomfortably full. Time for another Sale and Gift Day! We feel led to do something for Congo again, and have heard from Gordon that a photocopier is urgently needed for the Bunia Theological Seminary. £800 needed, but £300 already to hand. So, £500 to raise.*

– *End-April: Having so many good second-hand clothes, asked Wellesley Lodge Old Folks Home if I could do a couple of small 'sales' at nominal prices. The residents were thrilled, and £50 was raised. I have always asked God to confirm his will by giving one tenth of the required total. So, praise the Lord, – there was the tenth!*

– Early May: Many invitations out to local churches and friends. In the meantime I am praying that God will increase the £50 to £100 even before the sale. Over and over the words come "O woman, great is thy faith, be it unto thee even as thou wilt." Shared this promise with KH and together we praised God for His goodness and the assurance that our trust would be rewarded. Not long to go now before the Sale, in my Quiet Time I am asking the Lord to increase my faith in His mighty word.

– May 13th (just 3 days to go!): In Daily Light today:: "Without faith it is impossible to please Him ... for He is a rewarder of them that diligently seek Him." (Heb. 11.6) The Sale and all the work looms ahead like a mighty challenge to faith and endurance. In 'Our Daily Walk': "I will take the cup of salvation and call upon the Name of the Lord" (Ps. 116.13). His sufficiency, His help. "I will go in the strength of the Lord God." "Speak unto the children of Israel that they go forward." And in Daily Light: "When ye stand praying, forgive if ye have ought against any." (Mk. 11.25) A solemn warning. Had a special cleansing time of prayer about two or three people whom I find extra awkward – Forgive! Read a quotation from Dr. Andrew Murray: "When you have a promise from God, it is just as much as a fulfilment. A promise brings you into direct contact with God. Honour Him by testing and obeying the promise. The disciples waited and prayed; they expected God to do something! It is not enough to believe. Believe and trust, then look to Him to give the blessing!"

– May 15th (day before the Sale): £100 in before the sale – Glory to His Name!

– May 16th (day of the Sale): Post at breakfast brought in a cheque

for £50 from a friend, – 'To start off your Sale!' Praise God for this big encouragement! Many visitors for the Sale. Colin and I busy serving coffee helped by several willing folk, and as usual we urged people to visit the "Bargain Basement" upstairs! By the end, a total of £600 in!

– Early August: Photocopier all paid for, tested and working, ready for shipment to Bunia!

The Sale and Gift Days have been a great challenge to my faith and the means of much blessing both in my own life and in the lives of others. A young lady from Madagascar was enabled through the Sales to come to Britain for training with YWAM and is now back in her country serving God. Another rather exciting project was to buy an electrocardiograph for my doctor son Malcolm in Malawi. Two sales realised the necessary funds and you can imagine our delight when the precious machine arrived at our front door in its polystyrene container all ready for despatch. My pleasure turned to consternation, however, as I realised we still had to get it to Malawi in Africa! As I cast this burden on the Lord, He directed me to contact British Airways' Managing Director and asked him what could be done and how. He was very interested and said, "I think BA would be able to see it safely into the hands of Dr. Molyneux himself—free of charges!" What a thrill it was when, only one week later, the electrocardiograph was handed over to Malcolm at Queen Elizabeth Hospital, Blantyre, Malawi—ready for immediate use. How we praised God for that great provision!

I have always found that it is as we exercise faith in God in specific ways that we find Him to be faithful. All too often we do not have because we do not ask God. (James 4:2) When we do ask, He gives. This in turn encourages us to trust Him more, and so our faith grows, bringing glory to God and blessing to others.

14

The Harvest is Past

My husband Colin had a great love for the Bible, the Word of God, and used to spend much time prayerfully studying it. He was often invited to preach at church services, and would prepare for many days and with great care and much prayer. People would quite often say to him, "Colin, I remember when you came to speak at our church twenty years ago, and I still remember what it was you preached about", or "Let me tell you, Colin, the text you preached on when you spoke at our church back in the early 70's!".

What was it about Colin's preaching that made such an impression on people? It certainly wasn't that he spoke loudly or with dramatic gestures. In fact, he very seldom raised his voice. Many felt that he had an anointing from God, and that there was in his preaching an authority that came from God and affected people. People often said of him that he had a close walk with God; what he said was what he really believed and lived in his own life. He also had a gift of using vivid, graphic language so that people could visualise the incident or situation in the Bible story that he was talking about and they felt they could identify with the characters or circumstances in the Bible passage. Colin's preferred method of preaching was to choose a text, preferably a short verse or even part of a verse, and then approach it and illustrate it from several different angles, and come back to the text again and again until it was impossible to forget it.

His keen sense of humour often came through as he preached. But there was never any sense of frivolity or levity. You had the sense that here was a man talking from the heart about the things that matter most of all.

God greatly blessed and expanded the work of the INF during the 16 years that Colin was General Secretary, and has continued to do so since. From being a very small Mission with its office in a front bedroom in our home, it has grown to have over 80 serving personnel today.

The sermon reproduced below (in summarised form) was preached back in 1987. Of course, Colin didn't realise when he preached it that morning that in just two short years his life here on earth would be over and he would be with the Lord. But none of those who listened could fail to sense how deeply and how urgently he felt about what he was preaching.

The harvest is past

The other day, as I was passing through farmlands and fields, I noticed how bare those fields looked. Only recently those same fields had been full of beautiful golden corn; now they stood brown and empty… and I thought of that verse "The harvest is past…" (Jer. 8.20)

Yes, only a few weeks previously those fields of corn had been ripening; there had been all the anticipation and the planning and the excitement as the time of harvest drew nearer and nearer – and now, almost suddenly, that harvest was past. How like so much in our lives: pleasures and fears, joys and anxieties, holidays and responsibilities, happy prospects and dreads… and so on and so on. They all loom so large and fill our horizon as we prepare and draw nearer to what awaits us, full of delight or maybe dread; then, so quickly, it is all past and gone. As the Bible puts it so concisely: "It came – to pass."

In fact, that is the context of the verse in Jeremiah: "The harvest is past, the summer is ended, and we are not saved." It's so easy to think that some time soon we will trust the Lord, believe that that death He died on the Cross was for us and seek His forgiveness and be saved -- and all of a sudden it will be too late: the Harvest will be past. How unbearably, unthinkably tragic it will be for some who have every intention of being saved before long, suddenly to find "Oh, the Harvest is past: It's all been gathered in – and I, I'm not saved! I am not among the saved ones: they have all been gathered in and now the Gospel invitation is over; it's past."

How foolish of the governor, Felix, to say to the Apostle Paul, "When I have a convenient season ..."

How wise of the Bible to say, "Today is the day of salvation."

One day (none of us know when) the cry will go up: "The Harvest is past!"

Yes, it only seemed like yesterday when there was all that yellowy, golden corn rippling softly in the breeze – now, the harvest is past. Perhaps some had been wanting to help in bringing in the corn, glad to lend a hand with all this wonderful harvest. They should have acted, not just thought about it: it's too late now; the harvest is past.

Surely it was this same sense of urgency that our Lord was displaying when He said, "I must work .. while it is day: the night is coming when no man can work." I remember some while ago, out on the hills of Nepal, seeing the whole family working on and on as fast as they could, bringing in the rice harvest, and even when night came on they still worked by the light of small paraffin flares. Every member of the family was roped in, and how they all worked! They must bring in the crop before the weather changed, for then the harvest would be past. Twice in his epistles the Apostle Paul exhorts us that we should be "redeeming the time".

When this cry "The Harvest is past" goes out in that Day there will be those who will say, "I had wanted to do so much for the Lord, but I kept putting it off. I had all sorts of plans where and how I would serve Him but I couldn't bring myself to take the actual step of faith. It's too late now. The Harvest is past." Perhaps the servant in that very telling parable in Luke 19 had every intention of putting the money into the Bank: he was going to do it any day now ... and then, unexpectedly, the King came and it was too late. It was all being gathered in; in fact, the Harvest was past.

Perhaps this was another reason why Paul burst out with, "Woe is unto me if I preach not the Gospel." The Lord Jesus said to His own, "Pray to the Lord of the Harvest, that He would send forth labourers into His Harvest..." and we have been meaning to pray that, even to go ourselves, but we never really got round to it; and one day (how soon, I wonder?) it is going to be said that the Harvest is past now.

As I stood looking around on that beautiful, sunny October day, how lovely it all was! True, the harvest with all its bustling about and all its activity was over – but what beauty still! The vivid blue sky, those exquisite golds and browns, yellows and reds and then the dark green of the woods: what a glorious sight! No work going on any more, but what glory! Such quietness, such beauty that we said to one another, "It all just speaks of the Lord". No work, but what glory. Does this describe some in our fellowship? All the activity and the much busyness for the Lord is past now because of illness or old age or infirmity, but oh, how He is glorified in that beautiful life that speaks so clearly of Him. As Paul exclaimed, "... that the life of Jesus might be made manifest in us, in our mortal bodies." Praise God, when physical strength and energy fail there are still His beauty and His peace – yes, and all the fruit of the Spirit, as we obey Him and as the Holy Spirit fills us – that we can show forth in our lives.

How much, it will be found, has been gathered in for our Lord in that way when at last that Day comes and the Harvest is past?

Just two years after this sermon, Colin's heart attacks became more frequent. On 29th October, 1989 (Sunday) we woke early and I realised that Colin looked very pale and not quite himself. While we sipped our early morning cup of tea I said to Colin, "Our son Colin John will be preaching today out in Madagascar, and this is his birthday. Did you realise that?" And as I said it a solemn thought came to my mind preparing me that <u>this</u> day my dear one would go <u>Home</u>. Although he was not feeling well, he insisted on going to church as usual... but I had misgivings in my heart. As we sat in the morning service, the words of the opening hymn by John Newton appeared on the overhead screen—

1. Why should I fear the darkest hour
Or tremble at the tempter's power?
Jesus vouchsafes to be my tower.

2. When creature comforts fade and die
Worldlings may weep, but why should I?
Jesus still lives, and still is nigh.

3. I know not what may soon betide
Or how my wants shall be supplied
But JESUS knows, and will provide.

4. Against me earth and hell combine;
But on my side is power divine;
Jesus is all—and HE IS MINE!

Everyone in the big church was singing the words, but as I sang it seemed as if the words had special meaning, particularly verse 3. I believe Colin found them significant too, because we exchanged glances and squeezed each other's hands. I knew in my heart that my dear husband was going to be promoted to the peace and joy of Heaven, and there was a wonderful assurance that the Lord was indeed going to uphold us in His everlasting arms.

Arriving back home for lunch, Colin had to stumble with help up the stairs and straight to bed, exhausted and with pains in his chest. The doctor came along and gave injections, called the ambulance and sent him straight to casualty. In spite of shock treatment, his life quickly ebbed away, and at 5 p.m. he died suddenly. A dear friend, Dr. Lambert, came immediately to support me. But inwardly I had amazing peace and comfort from the Lord. We went back to my home in Ewell to pick up things for an overnight stay at the Lamberts. Before leaving the house I went to Colin's office to make sure everything was all right. There on an empty desk were Colin's "Last Will and Testament", and a lovely little card written in his own writing—

> "I, the Lord, will hold thy right hand, saying unto thee—fear not, I will help thee."
>
> Isaiah 41.13

Quite obviously, God had prepared us for this parting.

My son Malcolm came as soon as possible from Liverpool to help me with funeral arrangements. We notified Colin in Madagascar, Gordon in Congo and David in Sweden. The funeral service was held at Cheam Baptist Church—and we were wonderfully supported by loving friends in a full church. Gordon was the only son who could not get to England on time,—the message only reached Congo on the day of the funeral itself. But it was better, really, because he and Christine and the two little girls arrived from Congo and gave more valuable help and support at a time when it was particularly needed.

It was a time when inevitably many daunting and bewildering questions were going through my mind. How could I possibly manage? Where would I live? It was not long before God provided a beautiful little bungalow in sheltered accommodation in the very village near Loughborough where my son Colin and his wife Christine live. I have proved the on-going truth of those words that were so meaningful back in 1989: *I know not what may soon betide, or how my wants shall be supplied, But JESUS knows, and will provide*. Praise God!

Life has inevitably been very different without Colin. Together, through all sorts of experiences in different countries, we had proved that God can be trusted. We were just six weeks short of our Golden Wedding anniversary when Colin went to be with the Lord. Since then I have had to prove God's faithfulness and strength in new ways and have found His love and provision just as constant and dependable as when Colin and I were together. When everything around changes, He remains the same.

Epilogue
Look Forward with Joy!

This little "book of remembrance" is almost finished. Only a fraction has been written down, and the process of recalling and writing has, in turn, awakened all sorts of other memories, too numerous to include here. But enough has been recorded to demonstrate the goodness and the faithfulness of God.

As I look back over all the years since those early childhood days in Angola, what a lot has happened, and how full and interesting life has been! To bring the story up to date, Colin John, our first son, having completed mechanical engineering training, went on to the Faith Mission in Edinburgh, and met his bride-to-be Christine at a Faith Mission campaign where she was a leader. They went out together to serve in Congo, amazingly returning to Booke itself for three years, and then joined the Africa Inland Mission to serve in north-western Kenya. After a number of years, they moved, with their two children, to Madagascar for ten years before taking up their present appointment representing AIM in the north of Britain.

Malcolm, our second son, along with his consultant-paediatrician wife Elizabeth, spent several years at Queen Elizabeth Hospital in Blantyre, Malawi, then took a teaching post at the Liverpool School of Tropical Medicine, and has majored in research into malaria. They divide their time between Liverpool and Malawi. They have four children.

The third son, Gordon, went out to north-east Congo with UFM Worldwide for a ministry of theological education over a period of 21 years. About halfway through that time, while back in England, he met his wife Christine (at that time a sister tutor at St. Thomas' Hospital, London). During their later years in Congo, they adopted their two Madagascar-born daughters. Currently, Gordon is a lecturer/tutor at All Nations Christian College where my husband Colin studied 60 years ago!

It was at All Nations that our fourth son, David, did his training, before going out to Nigeria with the SUM combining agriculture and Bible-teaching. While back in Britain on home assignment, he visited his brother Gordon who was home from Congo being treated for filaria in the London Hospital for Tropical Diseases. David fell in love with the nurse who was attending to Gordon. David and Solweig later got married, and did further missionary service in Zambia during which time God blessed them with three sons. David subsequently accepted an invitation to pastor a church in Sweden.

How wonderfully God has protected and provided for all four families right up to the present time!

It has been a pleasure for me to have you "looking back with Joy"! But I am also glad that this little book does not need to be only looking back. As Christians, no matter how wonderful and rich the past may have been, we do not need merely to look back or dwell in the past. Christ is going before us, ahead of us, and we follow Him. We know He has conquered death, and we know that the best is yet to be. No matter how uncertain the future is, we know that the future is in His hands. He has promised to be with us always, right to the very end, and His promise is that He will never leave us or forsake us. His faithfulness in the past is guarantee of His trustworthiness in the future.

My sons often tease me because my motto is, "Life's too short!" I usually quote that saying as an excuse to live life to the full, enjoying every moment because no opportunity should be lost. But however long or short life may be (and none of us knows what it will be for us) the best thing is to live it for Him!

How long ago it seems now, that stormy night in Canada when as a little girl I asked Jesus into my heart and declared that I wanted to be a missionary to Africa! Looking back, I have no regrets that I gave to God what really belonged to Him anyway,—my whole life. And because my life is in His hands, I can now look forward with joy!

I hope you can, too.